DF77
A52

THE GREEK MIND

WALTER R. AGARD

Professor of Classics
University of Wisconsin

AN ANVIL ORIGINAL

under the general editorship of

LOUIS L. SNYDER

D. VAN NOSTRAND COMPANY, INC.

PRINCETON, NEW JERSEY

TORONTO   LONDON

NEW YORK

To

SEELYE BIXLER, EVERETT GLASS, and
PAUL TRAVIS,
who, like Solon of Athens, remain young in spirit

D. VAN NOSTRAND COMPANY, INC.

120 Alexander St., Princeton, New Jersey
257 Fourth Avenue, New York 10, New York
25 Hollinger Rd., Toronto 16, Canada
Macmillan & Co., Ltd., St. Martin's St.,
London, W.C. 2, England

*All correspondence should be addressed to the
principal office of the company at Princeton, N. J.*

Library of Congress Catalog Card No. 56-12902

PREFACE

SINCE there are many excellent anthologies of ancient Greek literature and countless volumes on Greek life and thought, what justification can there be for this book? In addition to the obvious fact that it is concise and convenient, two further claims may perhaps be made: first, that the readings and interpretations are grouped and correlated in terms of certain basic problems and patterns of life; second, that all of the translations are in a contemporary idiom.

With a wealth of material available for the Readings, my problem has been one of the most rigorous selection. I have chosen passages which are representative of the Greek mind and which seem especially pertinent to us today, including such subjects as international relations and the rights of minorities. The translations are my own, with the one exception noted below. In them I have tried to render the Greek (sometimes compressed, I regret to say, for lack of space) in a modern idiom which is fair to the original meaning. A further explanation should be made of the fact that, with one slight exception, no poetic translations are included; the lyric and dramatic excerpts are rendered in prose. This is certainly unjust to the poems and plays, but I am inclined to think that verse translations are more unjust. Poetry is a marriage of music and idea; and it is impossible to recreate in a different language the sound and rhythm of any poem. Rather than give a distorted version of the musical element, I have been content to translate the bare ideas. In that way one may see the *mind* of the poet at work, even though the music which makes his ideas so much more emotionally stirring is lost.

There are only a few selections from the tragedies and comedies included in the Readings. A play should be read in its entirety; passages torn from their context lose much of their relevance. The one scene given at some length, from Euripides' *Medea,* has the advantage

3

of being easily understood and felt "across the footlights of the centuries."

One final word of warning. Any such compressed account as this is bound to suffer from oversimplification. The remedy is to read widely in such original sources and commentaries as are suggested in A Short Bibliography at the end of the book.

For permission to reprint brief excerpts from some of my previous publications I am indebted to the University of Kansas Press (*The Humanities for Our Time*), the University of North Carolina Press (*What Democracy Meant to the Greeks*), and the University of Wisconsin Press (*Classics in Translation*, Vol. I). I am further indebted to the University of Wisconsin Press and to my colleague, Herbert M. Howe, for permission to use his rendering in *Classics in Translation* of the passages concerning Archimedes (*Reading No. 21b*).

Madison, Wisconsin   WALTER R. AGARD

TABLE OF CONTENTS

Part I

THE GREEK MIND

FOREWORD

WHY *THE* GREEK MIND?

Two questions are immediately suggested by the title of this book: What right has anyone to speak of *the* Greek mind, and, if such a thing did exist over 2000 years ago, why should people in the twentieth century concern themselves with it?

Can one with any precision say *"the* Greek mind"? Certainly during the centuries of the recorded culture of ancient Greece there were countless different minds in various times and places. Which time and place should be chosen? Mycenae in the heroic age, when Agamemnon was said to have led an expeditionary force against Troy? Lesbos in the sixth century B.C., when Sappho wrote her poems? Fifth-century Athens during the days of a peaceful and prosperous democracy? Or during the attempts at federal union, or the sophisticated society of cosmopolitan first-century Alexandria? The differences are so great that we may well question whether any significant common denominator can be found. And then the further question arises: What kind of people are to be chosen? Shall they be professional philosophers and scientists, or statesmen, businessmen, farmers, artisans, housewives? Here again there was such a tremendous range in intellectual capacity, interests, and achievement that we might conclude that it is useless to attempt such a generalization.

And yet, perhaps to make the attempt is useful. We constantly speak of "the American way of life," a term that is open to the same objections. It has, none the less, a fairly definite meaning and a practical value in stirring Americans to thought and action. It means ideally that equal opportunity is available to all to develop and utilize

their abilities, enjoying the freedoms provided by the
Bill of Rights. Of course many Americans have not subscribed to this belief, even in theory; there have always
been other American ways of life. And among those who
have subscribed to it in recent years, the tendency has
been to confine it to economic opportunity. Certainly in
practice the ideal has been far from realized. Yet to
question that the phrase has genuine and important meaning would be a serious error.

Can any similar general point of view be determined
in the thinking of the ancient Greeks? The attempt is
worth making; but at the start it should be clear that
we have no desire to be classified with the "society of-
fender" on the Lord High Executioner's list in the
Mikado—"The idiot who praises with enthusiastic tone/
All centuries but this, and every country but his own."
Whatever value the analysis may have will be in terms
of its helping us to meet the problems of our time and
offering us some aid in our search for happiness.

Using as the chief basis what is generally regarded as
the culmination of Greek culture, that created by Athens
during the fifth and fourth centuries B.C. (in this book
dates will be B.C., unless otherwise specified), but including also characteristic men and movements from
other periods and places, we may say at least that the
prevailing Greek *attitude* of mind, and by no means only
that of the intellectual giants, was a freely inquiring one,
which enjoyed experimenting with a wide variety of
speculation and activity, and had a robust faith in the
rational control of experience. Few societies have encouraged intellectual curiosity about the nature of the
world, social and political institutions, and the capacities
and limitations of men, as zestfully as the Greeks did.
Few have been so varied, enjoying a polytheistic religion,
many types of government, and many forms of art (not
only what is today called "classical," but also realistic,
romantic, impressionistic, baroque, and to some extent
even abstract art). And few have been so confident of
the capacity of men to attain by rational means the good
life, relatively free from authoritarianism of any kind.

That confidence was basically a reliance on plain common sense. The most popular of all Greek maxims was

the one emphasized at Apollo's shrine at Delphi, "Nothing to excess," and elaborated upon by poets, statesmen, and philosophers. This was no prescription, however, for anemia; instead, it was a necessary corrective for over-abundant vitality and emotional drive. "Boundary" was also a favorite word; Greeks generally preferred to limit situations and ideas to those which could adequately be comprehended by their intelligence; they disliked vagueness, uncertainty, and mysticism. As far as uncommon sense was concerned, a similar attitude prevailed: the attempt was made by statesmen and philosophers to determine by objective reasoning what was right conduct for both individuals and states. It is significant that ethics played a small part in Greek religion; codes of conduct were determined by reflecting on the trial and error of social experience. That is not to say that there were not many irrational beliefs and practices among the Greeks. As E. R. Dodds has brilliantly demonstrated in his recent book *The Greeks and the Irrational,* they had plenty of them, although there were more in the early and late periods than in the Great Age. But even in that period the tragedians pictured neuroses and complexes which have provided names for modern psychiatry. This is, of course, a relative matter; and perhaps all that should be said is that many Greeks tried unusually hard to be rational, and enjoyed the attempt. They also had, it should be added, a lively sense of humor.

Regardless, however, of the value of these general attitudes (and their value has often been questioned), how can people today profit from the specific experience of the ancient Greeks? Here are five possible ways.

1. The Greeks were remarkably like us in many of the problems they faced and the solutions they tried. In fact, much of the cultural pattern of our Western institutions is Greek in origin; and we can understand our pattern better when we see how and why it began. Our climate of free inquiry was first established by Greek scientists and philosophers. Democracy was first formulated in theory and put into practice in Greece. Many of our forms of literature and art have followed a Greek tradition. And our major philosophies are derived from Greek prototypes. By seeing these similarities in a setting

so different from our own we may find the familiar values
freshly minted.

2. In many ways the Greek mind was different from
ours. The recognition of contrasting values is important,
because it enables us to understand our own culture
better and may suggest improvements in it, freeing us
from the prevailing prejudice that everything present is
better than anything past. The most obvious difference
is that whereas our age is above all else characterized by
and dependent on the technological devices of practical
science, in this respect the Greeks were quite primitive.
They learned how to be civilized, some one has said,
without being comfortable. Placing the two cultures side
by side, we are bound to ask how important such aids
to comfort and communication really are.

Another major difference is that whereas our society
is dominated by business methods and standards, Greek
society devoted time and gave prestige less to them and
more to political activity. In Athens many of the leading
businessmen were not even citizens. Advertising, cutthroat
competition, and the appeal to top-flight minds of careers
in commerce and industry, played a less important role
then than now, and political careers had a more ex-
hilarating appeal. Finally, whereas we claim to be by
and large a Christian civilization, the Greeks were pre-
Christian.

3. One of the chief problems raised by Greek statesmen, dramatists, and philosophers was the proper balance
between the individual and the community, between freedom and authority. What were the obligations of people
to their city-states, and of the states to their citizens?
What were the necessary limitations placed on individual
liberty, and what ones were unnecessary and intolerable?
How about minority rights? These are still crucial questions. Past experience in answering or failing to answer
them should help us.

4. "Those who cannot remember the past," George
Santayana once said, "are condemned to repeat it." History is worth studying quite as much for the failures it
records as the successes. In one notable respect the
Greeks failed tragically: in international relations. To
their credit it should be said that they tried many devices

to secure independence and peace: isolationism, defensive alliances, a balance of power, empire, leagues of city-states. None succeeded for long, and the states finally fell into the grip of a totalitarian power because of their inability to unite. How and why the various attempts failed may have relevance to twentieth-century nations still striving for independence and peace.

5. Finally, in our individual search for self-respect and happiness in the face of a harrowing atomic age, we may find in the comradeship of Greek minds and the achievements of Greek culture some understanding, comfort, and, perhaps, inspiration. For in this humanistic field, unlike that of science, the achievements of earlier times are not to be discarded as inferior; the sensitive insights into human motives realized by Greek poets and dramatists are still relevant, the faith in human decency and the courage of philosophers and statesmen still challenge us, the radiant serenity of classical Greek art may still calm and uplift our spirits. All this is a vital part of the intellectual, aesthetic, and moral treasury of our Western world, and we shall impoverish ourselves if we disregard it.

To the people of the United States any such impoverishment would be especially tragic. Inasmuch as the United States has assumed the industrial, financial, and military leadership of the Western world, there is need for an increased understanding of the cultural traditions of that world if we are to provide leadership worthy of the name. And when the phrase "defending Western civilization" is used, it will have little meaning if the defense is thought of merely in military and economic terms. This is not to say that only the Mediterranean-European culture is of importance to us; such a provincial attitude would be equally tragic in a world wherein the great traditions and achievements of the Orient demand our sympathetic understanding, if we are to win confidence and respect as an international leader. But it remains true that the foundations of our indigenous culture are Mediterranean-European, consisting primarily of the religious and moral insights of the Jews and the intellectual, aesthetic, and ethical experience of the Greeks. That is our native environment of values, represented by the uninhibited use of the critical faculty, the exercise of political responsibility, sensitiveness to clarity of form, and uncompromising respect for human dignity and freedom. These are the attitudes which the Greek mind, if we are receptive, can communicate to ours.

— 1 —

PIONEERS: THE SETTING

The Physical Environment. The development of the Greek mind was caused by many factors, but among them the influence of the physical environment must be considered important. Greece was the stepping stone from Asia to Europe, the bridgehead by which the earlier great cultures of Asia Minor and Egypt moved westward. The Aegean Sea, with its scores of islands, encouraged exploration and the exchange of ideas as well as of material goods. The land was a country of limestone and marble mountain ranges, with narrow valleys between them; the soil was thin, favorable chiefly for the cultivation of olive orchards and vineyards; there were few mineral deposits. The climate, sunny and neither oppressively hot nor cold, was suitable for outdoor activity nearly all the year round. Insofar as physical surroundings affect human character the Greeks might be expected to have been healthy, hard-working, and venturesome, molded by the sun, the mountains, the poverty-stricken soil, and the sea; clear-sighted and practical, rather than moody or mystical, since the landscape was one of sharp outlines, strong colors, and well-defined forms. There was variety in the scene to stimulate versatility in the people. If the mountains provided protection for the development of independent city cultures, the sea saved them from provincialism. Finally, there were the geometry and color of the Mediterranean landscape to encourage the aesthetic sensitivity of the people living there. Lacking overpowering grandeur and mystery, it had fine proportions and clarity of form to stimulate the

15

eye and mind. Without laying too much stress on geographical factors, we may see in them a strong formative influence on the attitudes and values cherished by the Greeks.

Tribal Invasions. Descending during the second millennium B.C. upon the people living in this northeastern Mediterranean area there came wave after wave of invaders from around the Danube basin, part of that migration of Indo-Europeans who swept ultimately westward across all Europe. They were sturdy fighters, a robust, youthful race, who subdued the indigenous population, many of whom were culturally far superior to them, as archaeological excavation in Crete has demonstrated. How the Ionian and Achaean tribes profited from the Mediterranean cultural influences is evidenced by discoveries made at such sites as Mycenae and Pylos. It was the amalgamation of these two ethnic stocks (Mediterranean and Alpine, the anthropologists call them) and their customs which produced the people and ways of thinking that we call Greek.

Political and Economic Exploration. Following the tribal age there was a long period of adjustment to the problems of peaceful living. Then, from 700 to 500, came rapid commercial and political development, with a consequent impetus to cultural change. This was the time of Greek adolescence, when men felt the exhilaration of curiosity, growth, and delight in a new, rapidly unfolding world. Independent city-states grew strong, with workers and businessmen challenging the power of the nobles. There was steady expansion in industry and commerce to supplement the earlier agricultural economy. Economic problems of the farmers were partly solved by a colonization movement; hundreds of settlements to the northeast, south, and west were peopled by emigrants from Greek cities and soon created a flourishing life of their own, thus relieving congestion at home and opening new sources of supplies and markets all over the Mediterranean area. International athletic and religious festivals were established. Artists and writers made visible and articulate the aspirations of the people. The tribal hero had now given way to the responsible citizen of the city-state.

PIONEERS: MAN, NATURE, AND GOD

The Olympian Gods. The northern tribes worshipped a family of gods representing for the most part the upper air and sky, whereas the chief divinities of the southerners seem to have been earth and underearth spirits. Integration of the two religions resulted in a multiplicity of divinities, but the supreme god was the northern Zeus, "father of gods and men," whose family was supposed to live at the top of Mount Olympus; they were known as the Olympian gods.

Relation of Gods and Men. A basic belief of the early Greeks was that the present gods did not create the world, but came fairly late in the evolution of forms out of the original Chaos. (*See Reading No. 1a.*) They were regarded as having more or less control over the world and human affairs, but as probably being themselves subject in ultimate decisions to Destiny. They had division of labor: Hermes, for example, was a messenger, Hephaestus a craftsman, Artemis a huntress. Zeus and his daughter, Justice, were supposed to be the special guardians of promises and the observance of custom. (*See Reading No. 1b.*)

The gods were regarded as being similar in nature to men, differing only in superior power, longevity, and beauty. By believing in such divinities the Greeks felt securely at home in a world governed by powers so like themselves. Their attitude may be summed up by the statement, "I give so that you may give"; men acknowledged the power of the gods, and hoped by sacrifice and prayer to avoid their anger and secure their good will.

17

Although there was often tender and reverent devotion
in the worship, it was primarily a business relationship.
There was no deep conviction either that the gods had
created mankind (various explanations were advanced
for man's existence), or had any great solicitude for
men's welfare, except as individuals by special offerings
or native ability won their favor. (*See Reading No. 1c.*)
The religion included no sacred book; although Homer's
Iliad and *Odyssey* and Hesiod's *Theogony* summed up
prevailing religious concepts, they had no sacred significance in themselves. It insisted on no creed; people
were free to accept any accounts of the gods that they
cared to. It had little ethical content; there was no precise code of conduct handed down from Mount Olympus.
It had no organized churches or comprehensive priest-
hood; there were countless priests of different cults, but
their responsibility was to perform the proper rituals of
sacrifice, prayer, and festival for whoever wished to
participate. There was no conflict between church and
state; religion was one aspect of community life, controlled by the government. The essential element in
Greek religion was ritualistic worship. It was a religion
of extraordinary tolerance and diversity. As such it penetrated into every aspect of Greek life: it was an interpretation of the natural world, a consecration of daily work
and of social institutions, and one of the chief sources of
inspiration for poets and artists.

Relation of Mythology to Religion. It is fortunate
that demands were not made on worshippers to believe
specific accounts of the gods, since in the extremely
varied mythology which developed there were many
instances of inconsistency in the stories and of immoral
conduct on the part of the divinities. Because of the
fusion of different religious strains, such variety was
inevitable. Some myths arose out of the early rituals
involving natural phenomena, such as stories of Demeter
and Persephone which personified the revival of vegetation in the Spring. Others represented important human
attributes, such as Hermes' business ingenuity; and since
in human affairs not all the powerful and successful
activities seemed to meet exacting ethical tests, so among
the gods exploits were pictured involving deceit and

cruelty. A third group of myths arose out of religious history; many of the love affairs of Zeus, for example, were stories based on the mingling of Olympian and Mediterranean cults during the time of the tribal invasions. And to this already complicated mythological web the story-tellers and poets added, as time went on, their purely fictional elaboration, until the mythology came to be regarded by thoughtful people as art or symbol rather than religious fact.

Life After Death. A shadowy existence for the soul in the underworld was the prospect for life after death. For nearly all people it was a painless existence; only a small portion of Hades was reserved for the punishment of outstanding sinners, like Sisyphus, and their sin was usually some personal affront to the gods. But the after-life was nothing for even a hero or a saintly man to anticipate with pleasure; life here and now was regarded as the desirable one. (*See Reading No. 1d.*)

The Mysteries. Beginning probably with the widespread economic distress of the seventh century another type of religion became popular in many parts of Greece, the so-called "Mysteries." When life here and now was so painful and seemingly so unfair, people turned to cults like those of Demeter, Dionysus, and Orpheus, which helped the initiates to endure their present suffering and enjoy the prospect of a blessed immortality. (*See Reading No. 1e.*) It should be noted that membership in such cults was in addition to the worship of the Olympian gods, not in place of it, thus adding to the diversity of Greek religion. The difficulties faced by the Dionysiac cult in making its way into Greece is the theme of a later tragedy by Euripides, the *Bacchae;* apparently at the start there was opposition, not so much from priests as from political leaders who feared the explosive character of these mystery cults. Later they were incorporated into the state religion.

The Questioning Mind. During the early sixth century in cities on the coast of Asia Minor, such as Miletus and Ephesus, a few men began to question the traditional explanations of the nature of the world and to ask radical and penetrating questions; they were as keen in exploring new ideas as their business contemporaries were in exploring new markets. The chief questions they asked were: Of what material is the world made? How can its complex appearance be explained? The earliest answers were in terms of a single substance or principle. Thales (c. 580) suggested water, since moisture is so pervasive and can take various forms under the pressure of cold or heat. Anaximines (c. 550) argued that it was air, which becomes fire when rarefied, and wind, cloud, water, earth and stone when condensed; he was the pioneer in explaining the universe purely in terms of physical law. Heraclitus (c. 500) believed that fire described it best, that it was constantly changing as a result of the conflicts of opposites, and that a principle of limitation (Destiny or Necessity) preserved equilibrium in the universe. A different explanation was offered by Pythagoras (c. 510) and his followers; they were interested in the form rather than the material, and concluded that the universe could best be understood in terms of mathematical formulas. Anaximander (c. 550), the first of the physical philosophers to postulate a universal law which keeps any finite part from becoming "unjust" through excess, also the first to determine the equinoxes and map out the earth, made the daring deduction that man had evolved from animals of a simpler species.

So answers of many sorts were being given; the answers themselves were not as significant as the fact that freely inquiring minds were asking such questions and establishing a new climate of speculative opinion. It should further be noted that, although most of the answers involved physical substance, the men who gave them were not, generally speaking, materialists. In their attempt to explain how matter assumes so many different forms many of them posited principles of order or design. They were far from being irreligious; renouncing the traditional anthropomorphic concepts, they worked out ones that seemed to them more rational and laid the foundations for a monistic faith. (*See Reading No. 2.*)

— 3 —

PIONEERS: HEROIC VIRTUES

The Homeric Hero. During the period of conquest by the northern tribes, certain standards of conduct were established, chiefly in terms of the contribution of tribal leaders to their people's welfare. These standards, at first aristocratic, were later incorporated into democratic education, since the epic poems were a basic part of later Greek elementary education.

The Iliad. Although there is still controversy regarding the date and authorship of the *Iliad,* probably an Ionian poet in the ninth century wove many of the traditional stories of the tribal invasions into a story fairly well unified around a central plot. Out of the legends he chose one episode, from the story of the ten-year Trojan War, which lasted only seven weeks and was not primarily concerned with battles: a quarrel between Agamemnon, the commander-in-chief of the allied tribes, and hot-tempered and lonely Achilles, leader of one of the tribes and by far the ablest fighter among either the Achaeans or Trojans. This episode he invested with tragic grandeur. Since both Achilles and Agamemnon put their personal pride ahead of the allied cause and the welfare of their fellow-soldiers, both had to become wiser through suffering; Achilles developed from adolescent irresponsibility to a measure of maturity as he mourned over his fallen friend, Patroclus, and pitied Priam, the father of Hector whom he had slain. Among the host of characters, such as kindly Priam, indolent Paris, and realistic, disillusioned Helen, in Troy, and resourceful Odysseus, aged Nestor, and gallant Diomedes among the Achaeans, Achilles is pre-eminently praised for his valor (*see Reading No. 3a*), and Hector for his mature responsibility and devotion to family and city. (*See Reading No. 3b.*) In his crisp imagery Homer shows typically Greek keeness of perception. He writes of an army seated "like a dark ruffled sea under the wind"; of a man falling in battle "like a poppy drooping heavy after showers of spring," of troops retreating "like goats fleeing before a storm," of the Trojan watchfires "like stars on a winter's night," similes "flowering, as it were, in the bloody and trampled plain of Troy."

The Odyssey. Whether the *Odyssey* was composed by the poet who wrote the *Iliad* is also disputed. But it certainly describes a later stage in social evolution and is much more intimate and romantic in mood. Ostensibly describing the return of Odysseus to his home in Ithaca after the capture of Troy, it actually is a tale of adventure and romance based upon the voyages of discovery and peaceful penetration along the Mediterranean following the aggressive tribal age. The author drew upon many traditional stories. Folklore is represented by the themes of the man who succeeds by using his wits, the absent husband and the faithful wife, "blood will tell" (Eumaeus the swineherd was a prince by birth), "beauty and the beast" (the shipwrecked Odysseus and Nausicaa), and the impossible journey (Odysseus goes to Hades). Sailors' yarns, based doubtless on actual experience but richly embroidered by the sailors' imagination, include the episodes of the Lotus Eaters, the giant Cyclops, the nymph Calypso, the witch Circe, the sea-monsters Scylla and Charybdis, and the Sirens. Homer himself, it may be surmised, introduced the central theme of resourceful Odysseus, the prototype of the successful businessman (he is always unblushingly acquisitive, and is taunted as a trader by one of the Phaeacian athletes), and the narrative frame at the beginning and the end based on the maturing of Telemachus, Odysseus' son. In this poem, in addition to the intellectual ingenuity Odysseus constantly displayed, thus making him then and in later times a very popular hero, another typical Greek virtue is illustrated: that of hospitality. It is portrayed in the most charming episode in the entire poem, the welcoming of Odysseus by the princess Nausicaa after he has been shipwrecked on the island of Phaeacia. (*See Reading No. 3c.*)

Heracles. There were many other heroes of the pioneer days, notably the legendary founders of various cities, such as Cadmus of Thebes, and gallant adventurers like Jason, Perseus, Castor, and Pollux; but a hero who soon transcended his local area and became universally admired and adopted was Heracles. Originally no more than a petty king of Tiryns, he became famous for his extraordinary strength, and to his original exploits of ridding the land of preying beasts and bandits were added, as time went on, many other adventures over wide areas in every direction, until he was known and celebrated by writers and artists as the foremost helper of mankind. He was thought of as much more than a man of strength. He had courage and determination; his exploits were performed for the public good, not for his own glory; he had a fair amount of modesty, tremendous zest for enjoying life, a robust sense of humor, and a great capacity for friendship. Also characteristic of this hero were his human limitations. He had no supernatural weapons; he relied on his own strength and used as weapons only his club and bow. His zest for life often led him to extremes in eating, drinking, and getting involved in love affairs; and once the burden of his labors was too much for him and he suffered a period of madness.

It may seem strange that such a pre-eminent Greek hero was not invested with outstanding intellectual powers. But the Greeks already had such a hero in Odysseus. And even in this respect Heracles was by no means negligible. Dealing with such problems as those of the regrowing hydra and the wrestler Antaeus, whose strength increased whenever he touched the earth, he was imaginative and keen-witted. His record of achievement was so great that, according to the legend, he won admission to Olympus as a demigod. More important, he won admission into the hearts of the Greek people as the outstanding example of qualities of leadership which they admired: physical vigor, courage, endurance, good humor, and devotion to public service.

— 4 —

PIONEERS: INDIVIDUAL VALUES

Free Speech. In the heroic age another typically Greek point of view became well established: the right of free speech for even common men. The tribal government was based upon a king, a council of nobles, and the common people; although the king made the final decisions, matters of importance were brought before a general assembly for discussion before action was taken. Here is the beginning of government with the consent of the governed. At one such assembly an ordinary soldier, Thersites, called upon the army to desert the commander, Agamemnon. (*See Reading No. 4a.*) He was humiliated because of it by Odysseus, but he was not prevented from voicing his opinions.

A Farmer Protests. After the heroic age there came the prosaic period of settling down and trying to make a living off the rocky soil of Greece. For a long period many of the small farmers suffered cruelly at the hands of the wealthier landowners. They found a spokesman in Hesiod (c. 750), himself cheated by a greedy brother and an unjust judge. In the first farmer's almanac, *The Works and Days,* he gave practical advice about farming, and included with it traditional lore, moral maxims, and wry humor. Among the traditional lore was the story of the five successive ages of mankind: gold, silver, bronze, the warrior heroes, and the present cruel age of iron; the last three of them had an historical basis. Hesiod also told the story of Pandora: how Zeus created woman to be men's plague. It was doubtless a reflection of the actual distress when there were several girls in a poor farmer's family for whom he could provide no marriage dowry. This prejudice against women constantly recurs later in more prosperous times, perhaps as a result of the influence of the Orient on Ionian Greece. In the sixth century a vitriolic satire by Semonides classified women as sows, foxes, meddlesome dogs, clods of earth, the variable sea; only a few, he said, were like the busy bee, and a man was lucky when he married one of them. On the positive side Hesiod preached a code of hard work, thrift, honesty, self-reliance, and religious observance as the only means of making the best of a hard life. (*See Reading No. 4b.*)

Aesop's Fables. Other expressions of the practical sense admired by ordinary people are the fables ascribed to Aesop (c. 650?). Such stories as those of the shepherd boy who cried "Wolf! Wolf!," the goose that laid golden eggs, and the dog in the manger, indicate what useful virtues honesty, moderation, and tolerance were considered to be. Many other fables taught similar homely lessons, especially the importance of facing disagreeable facts candidly. (*See Reading No. 4c.*)

The Oracle at Delphi. Moral and practical advice was given by the oracle of Apollo at Delphi, the chief international center of the ancient world. "Know thyself" (*i.e.*, your human limitations) and "Nothing to excess" were its chief maxims. The common sense of the oracle was shown in the replies it gave to individuals and states consulting it. Regardless of the hocus-pocus involving the medium who was supposed to be Apollo's mouthpiece, beyond question the priests knew what was going on in the world and had a shrewd understanding of the needs and capacities of people. They encouraged the founding of colonies to relieve overpopulation; their Pythian Festival, an all-Greek meeting not only of athletes but of political and cultural leaders as well, provided for the exchange of ideas in addition to competition in athletics and the arts; and the reassurance which the oracle gave to distraught individuals was usually based upon sound psychology.

Of the many oracular responses which are recorded in Herodotus' *History*, a touching one may be cited as typical. A young man named Battus from the island of Thera was worried over a speech defect, which he felt would keep him from realizing his ambition for leadership. So he made his way to Delphi to ask Apollo's advice as to how he could overcome it. Although he was surprised when the oracle told him to found a colony in Libya, he proceeded to organize a group and establish on the African coast the prosperous colony of Cyrene. Was his speech defect corrected? At any rate, the priests encouraged him to outgrow his nervous apprehension and have confidence in his ability to do something useful and important. The advice given cities was usually of the same sensible sort, although it was often couched in sufficiently cryptic terms to give the oracle an alibi in case disaster unexpectedly resulted. Of course at times events proved the priests definitely wrong, notably after they had advised the Athenians in 480 not to resist the Persian invasion; but even in that instance doubtless most people agreed with them that resistance, however heroic, would be futile. When the priests made mistakes it was usually, as on that occasion, due to a cautious conservatism.

   Business Skill and Tact.   The growing realization that intellectual ingenuity and the spirit of conciliation were necessary for success in business is delightfully illustrated in the *Hymn to Hermes,* a myth written probably about 650. (*See Reading No. 4d.*) It describes how on the first day of his life Hermes invented the lyre, stole Apollo's cattle, outsmarted that aristocratic god when he came to the cave-home of Hermes investigating the crime and then took Hermes up to Olympus to be tried before Zeus; and how Hermes finally got the good will of his opponent by making him a present of the lyre. In this tale there is a good detective plot, including the clever crime, the sleuth's seeking evidence, and the trial scene. But in addition there are meanings representative of the Greek mind in the pioneer period. It has the psychological significance of the little man overcoming his more privileged opponent by using his wits. It symbolizes the mercantile class (Hermes was their god) successfully challenging the power of the landed aristocrats, represented by Apollo, yet realizing that good will must also be established. And, finally, it sets a strong stamp of approval on intellectual keenness, even though it is employed unethically. Of course Hermes, the sharp dealer, was inferior to Zeus, the god of justice; but nonetheless his skill was positive and admirable.

Solon the Conciliator. The techniques of conciliation were used by the Athenian legislator Solon (c. 640–560) in a statesmanlike way, when, in arbitrating a crucial conflict between the rich landowners and the poverty-stricken farmers, he put to practical use the policy of the middle way, "so that neither side should have an unfair advantage over the other." His economic reform of canceling all debts which had resulted in personal slavery, and making it impossible for such security to be asked in the future, fully satisfied neither the rich, who wanted those debts paid to some extent, nor the poor, who asked for a complete redistribution of land. But it did remedy the acute disbalance of the Athenian economic structure. Realizing that such reforms would be only temporary unless positive political and economic measures were also adopted, he instituted people's courts to judge magistrates and encouraged the development of industry. And he stated and practiced for the first time the theory that government should be an impartial arbiter, reconciling conflicting interests. "Equality," he declared (meaning equality before the law) "breeds no revolution." When asked if he had enacted the best laws, he replied, "the best that could have been acceptable." The Greek virtue of moderation was never better practiced than by Solon. Nor the Greek attitude of youthful curiosity. In the *Timaeus* Plato reports an Egyptian priest, impressed by the aged legislator's unquenchable interest in new customs and ideas, declaring that there were no old men among the Greeks, since all of them remained young in spirit.

Solon's theory of arbitrating differences was followed to advantage in later fifth-century Greek domestic conflicts and interstate disputes; inscriptions show several instances where a neutral state was named to arbitrate disputes, and peace treaties regularly included a clause in which both sides agreed to submit their future disagreements to arbitration. Unfortunately in major disputes the principle was not often applied.

Pioneer Art. The fine arts mirror the spirit of en-

thusiastic exploration in humanistic values seen in so
many other fields during the sixth century. In architecture the Doric and Ionic styles were developed, with
many variations in plan, proportion, and decorative columns, friezes, metopes, and moldings; but in all of
them a normal human scale prevailed, and both the
grotesque and the grandiose were avoided. Sculptors,
as yet unable to portray the human form accurately,
invested somewhat schematized bodies with a fresh and
buoyant vitality, delighting in scenes from mythology
which represented gods and men in spirited action. Their
relief sculpture was notable for the clarity and vigor of
its geometric design. This was a prosperous period for
the vase makers and painters, since their art was in
great demand as one city competed with another in the
quality of its production of jars, pitchers, cups, plates,
and many other types of pottery. A vast number of
shapes for the various uses were experimented with, and
each dish had its individual decoration, with mythological
scenes again furnishing the chief subject matter, although scenes from everyday life were also popular.
Finally, about 525, the so-called red-figure technique
was invented. The figures were in terra-cotta color, delicate bristle-strokes sketched in the details, and the rest
of the vase was covered with lustrous blue-black glaze.
This permitted much more varied and lively movement
to be pictured than did the previous black-figure sil-
houette. Crisp linear precision characterized these illustrations. In other arts, such as gems, mirrors, dress, and
furniture, the same exploratory spirit and imaginative
design prevailed.

Poetic Insight. Along with political, commercial,
and artistic progress, speculation in physical philosophy,
and the growing independence of mind among ordinary
people, the seventh and sixth centuries also saw the
rise of talented individuals who invented lyric verse
forms to express their personal reactions to nature,
people, and situations. The fact that poets were now
voicing their own feelings rather than singing of the
heroic past is evidence of the new spirit of the times; and
in their emphasis on the pursuit of individual happiness
they contributed a liberalizing influence. Tyrtaeus (c.

650) praised patriotic devotion; Archilochus (c. 680) sang of the blither life of an independent soldier of fortune; Alcman (c. 630) wrote choral odes and hymns and made words, sounds, and rhythms mirror the emotions aroused by nature. Alcaeus (c. 580) wrote of civic strife and good fellowship, and Theognis (c. 540) commended the aristocratic code of honor. These are a few of the rising host of poets. The greatest of them was Sappho (c. 580), who conducted a girls' school honoring Aphrodite and the Muses on the island of Lesbos. Sensitive and intense, with deep feeling for her students, she found forthright and subtle expression for many moods, tender, satiric, passionate. (*See Reading No. 5.*)

In addition to the expression of individual moods and the invention of lyric forms for such expression, this poetry is distinguished in two other respects. First is the crisp economy of its phrasing, which may seem excessively austere to people used to poetic elaboration, but which stamps the image or idea with great precision on the reader or listener. Second is the richness of sound, a richness made possible by the extraordinary frequency of open vowels in the Greek language. One example may illustrate the point. When Sappho speaks of the "longing-voiced nightingale," the Greek sounds somewhat like this: eem-mer-o-phóne-os ah-áy-dough. There are actually three vowels and one consonant in the word for "nightingale," compared with four vowels and seven consonants in the English word; and whereas the English vowel sounds are high-pitched and thin, two of the Greek ones are full-bodied and deep, like the cello notes of the nightingale's song.

Changing Human Nature. Finally, toward the end of the sixth century in Athens, a most significant experiment in human relations was conducted which paved the way for the realization of greater opportunities for individuals in the following century. The leader of this experiment was Cleisthenes. Like so many political liberals he came from an aristocratic family, but he was quick to grasp the democratic trend of the times and chose to direct rather than oppose it. The first need was to destroy economic and political factionalism based on the old group loyalties. Cleisthenes worked out a scheme of registration which cut across the former divisions, each new unit including representation from the major economic and social classes. Thus by a shrewd administrative device people of different classes and conditions had to act in common, with the welfare of the entire city emphasized more than the interest of any single group. One can imagine that there was plenty of criticism on the ground that "you can't change human nature," but the simple fact was that human motives were educated and redirected by this administrative process. The new constitution adopted by Athens also provided for participation by more citizens in the government on a basis of equality, thus laying the foundations for the mature democracy of the Great Age. Hereafter all Athenian citizens would share in the control of their way of life. The pioneers had created conditions favoring dignity and importance for even the humblest man.

— 5 —

THE GREAT AGE: THE SETTING

The Creative Fifth Century. One of those dangerous but useful generalizations found in historical writing classifies the fifth century as primarily a creative period, the fourth century as chiefly critical. Certainly by any sensible definition there were creation and criticism in both periods; but perhaps in terms of a ratio there was some such difference. At any rate, the years from 500 to about 340 were years of greatness. The fifth century saw the repulse of the Persian invasions by temporarily united free states of Greece; this victory gave a tremendous lift to morale and a spur to community projects. It saw the formation of a federal union—the Delian League, an organization of more than two hundred city-states, most of them on the islands of the Aegean and the coast of Asia Minor, created to safeguard Greece from further invasions. It saw the rapid rise of Athens to economic and military leadership. It saw Athens, led by Pericles, prodigally productive in a score of ways: in developing democratic institutions, in a great building program, in drama and the fine arts, in historical writing, oratory, scientific medicine, and philosophy. Never during so short a time have so many men of unquestioned creative genius been active in one small area. Unfortunately war put an end to much of the creative spirit. After Athens had turned the Delian League into the Athenian Empire, a coalition of Sparta, Corinth, and Thebes in 431 challenged her power. Her control of the seas threatened Corinth's commerce; her successful democracy was regarded by the master-race oligarchy of Sparta as ideologically dangerous. The conflict, most of which was recorded in Thucydides' *History of the Peloponnesian War,* ended in the defeat of Athens in 404. Thereafter, she never regained her political and military power, although in the fourth century she continued to function as an economically successful democracy and for a while helped maintain a balance of power among the Greek states. Furthermore, much of Greece had suffered such physical and psychic wounds that the earlier creative zest was never recaptured.

The Critical Fourth Century.   If community enterprises were less distinguished than those of the former century, after 400 individual enterprises became more venturesome. Business firms flourished; artists received generous commissions from private patrons and developed new techniques of impressionism and dramatic and realistic sculpture; the comedy of manners supplanted the political comedy of Aristophanes; and schools of philosophy set to work on a much more thorough analysis of ideas and institutions than had previously been attempted. Notably the democracy of Athens, which had been so sure of itself in the previous century and had survived a terribly costly and lost war, came under attack by two of its products: Plato and Aristotle. And the time of the city-state as an institution was drawing to a close, with authoritarian Macedon looming from the north and finally bringing all of the Greek cities within its orbit.

— 6 —

THE GREAT AGE: MAN, NATURE, AND GOD

Aeschylus. A mature view of the evolution of religion was represented by Aeschylus (525–456). In his dramatic trilogy of the Prometheus legend (only the *Prometheus Bound* has been preserved), he pictured Zeus in his early days as an arrogant young god, relying on his superior power to crush without mercy rebels like Prometheus; but the final outcome (*Prometheus Unbound*) apparently pictured a Zeus grown wiser, more just, and willing to bargain. This was Zeus as fifth-century Athenians worshipped him. The concept of the gods had changed as the people's ethical principles developed. This attitude toward Zeus, defender of justice and Comforter, is beautifully portrayed by the chorus of old men in Aeschylus' *Agamemnon*, where they describe how Zeus as "hound of heaven" tracks the sinner down, call upon him as the sole consoler of those in bitter grief, and try to justify his ways to men. (*See Reading No. 6a.*) If men have to become wise through suffering, they say, the gods impose this bitter grace because they themselves went through the same sort of education. Aeschylus believed profoundly that the world is governed by a just Providence, which punishes arrogant pride but reconciles conflicting purposes.

Pindar. An optimistic view of heaven for those who win it by noble living was voiced by Pindar (518–438), the poet laureate of athletic odes. In his highly elaborate songs in honor of victorious athletes, Pindar took the actual event as merely a starting point, going on to praise the boy's ancestors and city, and mingling history,

mythology, and the glory of aristocratic principles of
honor. Now, according to his faith, a happy immortality
in the Isles of the Blest is available to men who have
lived nobly in this life. (*See Reading No. 6b.*)

   Sophocles and Euripides.   Although the tragedies of
Sophocles (496–406) have many references to the gods
(since the tragic writers based their plays on the heroic
legends it could hardly have been otherwise), the emphasis in them is upon the characters of the tragic men
and women rather than any divine agency. People in his
plays voice their duty to reverence the gods (*see Reading No. 11b*) and their recognition of divine power;
the influence of oracles and priests is recognized (although their motives are sometimes questioned); but
Sophocles was not primarily interested in problems involving religion. He was chiefly concerned with human
heroism and personal integrity in the face of any ob-
stacles—personal, social, or universal. If Sophocles was
not deeply concerned in his tragedies with conventional
religion, Euripides (c. 480–406) was positively critical
of traditional views regarding the gods. In his plays the
gods are pictured as heartless and brutal (Apollo in the
Ion, Dionysus in the *Bacchae,* Aphrodite in the *Hippolytus*); characters criticize them, or even question their
existence, and condemn priests and oracles; and mortals
often act on a higher level of ethics and kindness than
the gods are credited with. In this attitude Euripides
doubtless reflected the point of view of the skeptical
Sophists. His chief interest was in the relationships between individuals, especially those situations between
men and women which involved pathological factors.

   Physical Philosophers.   The cosmologists of the fifth
century continued their predecessors' search for physical
explanations of the universe, in a more systematic way.
Among them the following may be cited: Parmenides
(c. 450) of Elea, who took exactly the opposite position
from Heraclitus' theory of change, asserting that change
is simply an illusion of the senses and that the mind
assures us that only Being exists, unchanging and eternal;
the pluralist Empedocles (c. 493–c. 433) of Agrigentum,
who postulated four elements or "roots": earth, air, fire,
and water, as the indestructible materials out of whose

bringing together by Love and separation by Strife the forms in the universe are made; Anaxagoras (c. 500–c. 428) of Clazomene and Athens, a thorough-going materialist, who explained motion as being caused by an especially fine sort of matter with kinetic centrifugal power, which he arbitrarily defined as "mind"; and Leucippus (c. 440) of Miletus and Democritus (c. 420) of Abdera, both of whom proposed the theory that the universe is composed of atoms (indivisible particles) moving in empty space. (*See Reading No. 7.*) Democritus believed that these atoms are infinitely varied, and that Mind consists of very fine, fiery atoms; that there are many worlds, created by a cosmic whirl, a purposeless and purely mechanistic principle of causation.

Mathematics. "Let no one without mathematics enter here" was the motto of Plato's Academy; and Plato voiced the opinion of many intellectuals who considered mathematics essential in both elementary and the most advanced education. The foremost mathematician of the period was Eudoxus (c. 408–355). He created the theory of proportion applied to both commensurable and incommensurable magnitudes, and the method of "exhaustion" for measuring and comparing areas and volumes of plane and solid figures; he also attempted to explain by geometry the movements of the heavenly bodies, and solved the problem of doubling the cube.

Hippocrates, "Father of Medicine." Another indication of the inquiring spirit of the times was the research in medicine initiated by Hippocrates (c. 425). Counteracting popular belief in nonrational methods of treating disease, such as sympathetic magic, prayer and sacrifice, oracles, and amulets, Hippocrates believed that the careful study and recording of the circumstances involving any disease will permit the able physician to diagnose correctly and deal as effectively as possible with it. He established medical methods and a code of ethics for the profession which profoundly influenced later medical history. (*See Reading No. 7.*)

The Sophists. About the middle of the fifth century there came into prominence many so-called Sophists (wise men), traveling scholar-teachers who had enthusiastic followings, especially among the young men in Athens. They taught all sorts of subjects, including current scientific theories; but, in general, they took a dim view of the value of both religious and scientific interpretations of the world, believing that such speculation was purely theoretical and served no useful purpose. (*See Reading No. 8a.*) Most of their instruction was in the practical art of persuasive speech, the effective use of words, and methods of gaining success in public affairs. One of the greatest of them, Protagoras (c. 450) frankly acknowledged that he was an agnostic. "Man is the measure of all things," he declared. This has been interpreted as a statement of the relativity of knowledge, each man being his own authority on what is true; but it may represent a belief that human social judgments establish adequate rules of conduct. Among other Sophists, Gorgias scorned the study of the world of nature, declaring that nothing exists; if anything did exist we could not know it, and if we did know it we could not communicate the knowledge to others. Even more radical was Hippias, who advanced the theory of natural rights as opposed to social custom. Some of his followers developed the theory into a defense of strong individuals asserting their natural power regardless of custom or law: might, they declared, makes right. Such ideas caused grave concern among many of the citizens of Athens, who felt that the time-honored beliefs and moral standards were being undermined by these teachers. Their attitude is reflected in Aristophanes' *Clouds,* in which a caricatured Socrates and his disciples in a school called *The Thinkery* deny the existence of Zeus and the other conventional gods and worship instead such divinities as Clouds, Air, and Persuasive Tongue. Plato ridiculed the more superficial Sophists in his dialogue *Euthydemus.*

Socrates' Faith. The actual Socrates (469–399) was far from being either a materialist or a Sophist, if we may believe the account of his beliefs as given by Plato and Xenophon. In the *Memorabilia* of Xenophon he is pictured as religiously conventional; and in Plato's *Phaedo* he describes his early disillusionment with materialistic theories of Anaxagoras. (*See Reading No.*

8b.) He was hoping to find, he declared, an interpretation of the world in terms of intelligence directed toward a moral purpose. Such an interpretation he came to accept; and he believed that his mission of exposing ignorance and trying to discover the truth was divinely inspired.

Plato's World of Ideas. Socrates' greatest pupil, Plato, worked into a philosophical system the notion of the world which Socrates hoped was true, and in so doing set a pattern for later idealistic philosophy and religious faith. By elaborate analysis he arrived at the following conclusions. The world is dualistic. There is the material world which we apprehend to some extent through our senses; it is constantly changing and essentially unreal. And there is the world of Forms or Ideas, which we comprehend to some extent by means of our Mind; it is eternal, unchanging, and real. Just as men believe there is an actual physical world existing outside of themselves which corresponds more or less closely to their perception of it, so there is an actual world of Ideas, which corresponds more or less closely to their conception of it. How are they able to arrive at such concepts as Equality, Beauty, Justice, Truth? Plato made the suggestion that the mind of the individual must have existed in the world of Ideas before its existence in this material world, in order to be able to recollect these Universals. And upon the death of the body, he argued, the individual mind will again be at home in that world of Mind. (*See Reading No. 8c.*)

Aristotle on God and Nature. With the same essential faith as Socrates and Plato in a moral intelligence controlling the Universe, Aristotle (384–322) worked out an even more detailed system to demonstrate it. As a biologist he was more interested in the material world than Plato was; and although he accepted the Platonic conception of Ideas, he considered that they must be studied inseparably from matter. As a semanticist he analyzed the concept "causation" and applied his findings to the world: it is caused by its material, by the form the material assumes, by the agent who affects the form, and by the end purposed by the agent. There must be, he declared, a First Cause, the Prime Mover, God.

And there is always present the purpose which Mind intends matter to serve, although matter is often recalcitrant; the Universe expresses the purpose of a moral intelligence, whose own chief happiness consists in contemplation. Picturing this Ultimate Being, Aristotle, for all his logical and biological discipline, became quite as mystical as his teacher Plato. (*See Reading No. 8d.*) But in his zoological research Aristotle was highly realistic, showing accurate observation and analysis. Intensely curious about the whole natural world, he did invaluable service in recording the habits and structure of more than five hundred species of animals, including the heart and vascular system, traced the development of the chick, and made detailed studies of many marine forms. He was also the pioneer in scientific classification.

THE GREAT AGE: MAN
AND SOCIETY

Athens: Democracy and Empire. By the middle of the fifth century Athens had become the commercial, military, and cultural leader of the Mediterranean world, and the ruler of an Empire of some 200 city-states, although she still called them her "allies" in the Delian League. Here, for the first time, was a democracy governing an Empire. And until the stress of war brought out the brutal self-interest of Empire, Athens governed well.

Pericles. For about thirty years of comparative peace, between the repulse of Persia and the beginning of the Peloponnesian War, Pericles was the leader of the majority democratic party in Athens. Perhaps nowhere can history show a statesman of broader vision for his people. His range of interests was far wider than merely political, as a reading of Thucydides' *History* and the biography of him by Plutarch will show. He encouraged commerce and industry, science, and the fine arts. Himself a student of music and philosophy in his youth, he surrounded himself with the foremost scholars and artists of the Greek world; his closest friends were Anaxagoras and the sculptor Phidias. His great public works program remedied unemployment and added to the aesthetic prestige and happiness of the city; in statesmanlike fashion he realized that a great community is one profitably and joyously engaged in public enterprises which capture the imagination of the citizens. The only major weakness of Pericles was his imperial policy, which finally resulted in war. If he had favored

more generosity toward the so-called "allies" of Athens
and more restraint in the commercial and military expansion of Athens, it is conceivable that the disastrous
Peloponnesian War might have been avoided. But no
empires have been noted for such generosity and restraint. Thucydides sums up the character of Pericles in
glowing terms; no flatterer, he was willing even to pro-
voke the anger of the people; he retained their confidence because of his sound judgment, his liberal policies, and his personal integrity.

Pericles' Funeral Speech. After the first year of the
Peloponnesian War, at the state funeral for the fallen
soldiers Pericles gave an address which, in addition to
paying eloquent tribute to the dead, outlined the political
and cultural aims of the city which those men had died
to preserve. (*See Reading No. 9.*) It is obviously an
idealized picture, partly propaganda to help the morale
of the people; but it, nevertheless, expressed what Athens
on the whole wanted to be: a liberal democracy.

Democracy, Pericles said, means that power resides
with the majority of the citizens, not with any small
group. But the majority recognizes that all people deserve to have equal rights before the law, and that
individuals, regardless of their political, economic, or
social status, should have opportunity to receive recognition on the basis of their merit. He claimed that in
Athens there was respect for people's privacy and for
generally accepted unwritten as well as for formal laws.
As far as the procedure of government was concerned,
he declared that Athens believed in full discussion of all
measures before decisions were reached, in the conviction that free speech was essential if there was to be
wise action. In the same spirit no restrictions were put
upon foreigners coming to Athens and remaining there.

But Pericles went beyond the purely political advantages offered by the city, and elaborated upon its
cultural way of life. Athens, he declared, believed in
liberal education for all its residents, offering religious,
dramatic, musical, and athletic festivals throughout the
year, and public buildings "to cheer the heart and refresh the spirit as we see them every day." Along with
the advantages he also stressed the responsibilities.

Wealth, he said, was regarded as a means for public service rather than for private display. Men were expected to take their political duties seriously, and those who refused to do so were regarded, not as indifferent, but as "useless." The citizens must always remember that "happiness depends on freedom, and freedom is won and preserved by courage," and that Athens was made great by men who understood their duty and disciplined themselves to perform it well.

The Actual Democracy.   This is a noble speech, but how true is it to the facts of Athenian life? When the comparison is made, several explanations and reservations are in order. To begin with, when Pericles spoke of government by the majority, he meant only the majority among some 40,000 male citizens who had the right to vote. But in Athens there were some 25,000 resident aliens, 50,000 slaves, and the women, all of whom had no political opportunity. This was obviously a limited democracy. But it was by no means government by a specially favored leisure class. The 40,000 citizens represented no privilege of noble birth or economic position; they included a genuine cross-section of society, and fully half of them were in the lowest economic class of workers.

It was a direct democracy: the 40,000 voted in open assembly all legislation (like the traditional American town meeting). Nearly all the executive officers were chosen by lot from the registration lists and served only for one year; in this way one-party control and machine graft were made impossible, and a great number of the citizens were educated in political knowledge and practice. Legal matters were decided, not by professional judges, but by juries. All this indicates a faith in the judgment of the common man and a belief in the educative value of political liberty and equality. The rights of minority groups and individuals were generally respected, as Pericles claimed; and Athenian law won a well-deserved reputation for its fair dealing.

Politics as Education.   Pericles in his Funeral Speech declared that public service was recognized as a civic obligation. This was no mere rhetoric. It has been estimated that on any given day one Athenian citizen

in four was engaged in some form of service to the
State; and in the course of their lives most of the citizens would expect to have been on the executive council
or one of many official commissions, in addition to
voting regularly in the legislative Assembly. Thus, the
Athenian citizenry was educated in the understanding
of public affairs and in civic responsibility. The device
of selection by lot was largely responsible for this sharing
of community service. It certainly could not have been
expected to provide for securing the most experienced
and able public administrators, but it did guarantee a
high level of common knowledge and a wide range of
responsibility. The device of the lot was inherited by
the democracy from the aristocratic sixth century, when
it was used for two purposes: to settle disputes among
various aristocratic factions (no one can question a
decision determined by lot), and to make it easy for the
divine will to assert itself in human affairs. The democracy, by applying it to all the citizens, converted it into
a means of bringing the widest possible number of citizens into public service.

    Democracy in Law.   In the handling of legal cases
Athens further demonstrated her confidence in the sound
judgment of ordinary men. There were no professional
judges in our sense of the word, and no lawyers appeared in court; the principals involved had to present
their case directly to the jury, although lawyers may
have helped them prepare it. State officials chosen annually by lot for the duty of administering the courts
received indictments presented by individuals, and arranged the time and place of the trials. Then they drew
the names of jurors (sometimes as many as 501 for an
important case) from a panel of 6000 who had been
chosen by lot to serve as available for the year, and they
presided over the trials, merely as chairmen to guarantee
that proper procedure was followed. No charge was
given the jury. After hearing both sides of the case
presented by the principals and any witnesses they cared
to present, the jury voted on the question of guilt. If
the majority voted "not guilty," the case was dismissed;
if the prosecutor, however, failed to secure twenty per
cent of the votes he had to pay a substantial fine, the

purpose being to discourage people from bringing inconsequential or malicious suits and also to help meet the legal expenses of the city. If the verdict was "guilty," the jury chose one of two penalties—that proposed by the prosecutor, or an alternative offered by the defendant. The commonest penalty was a fine, and the next was exile; there was little imprisonment, and the death penalty was seldom invoked.

The informality of this procedure resembles what today would be considered parliamentary rather than judicial procedure. But it did show great confidence in the ability of ordinary men to render substantial justice. And, like political service, it educated many Athenians in a wide variety of social and economic problems.

Economic Enterprise. Athens had developed from an agricultural to a busy industrial and commercial city, judged in terms of its own time; but although many of its economic practices were similar to ours they were on a vastly smaller scale. It was a world, not of machines, but of handicraft, of limited resources and production, modest competition, virtually no advertising, and the mere beginning of a banking and credit system. Among the master-craftsmen and apprentices in each field there were organized guilds, which were primarily interested in good fellowship and improving professional standards of workmanship. Men who engaged in commerce took risks on every cargo. A normal rate of interest was twelve per cent. Such ways of doing business encouraged caution; economic security rather than profit venturing was the normal watchword.

Much of this business was carried on, not by the citizens of Athens, but by resident aliens. The citizens preferred to spend as much time as possible in the varied life of politics, athletics, religious, dramatic, and musical festivals and lively conversation. Yet they must not be thought of as a leisure-class people. Only a few of them did not have to work for a living, on farm, in factory, or on the sea; and fully half of them were day laborers.

In many ways Athens assumed responsibility for the economic welfare of its residents. The city owned and operated silver mines in the public interest. The wealthier people were called upon to make donations ("liturgies") for public purposes, such as the construction of naval vessels and the production of musical and dramatic festivals. Duties were levied on exports and imports, and imported wheat was kept at a reasonable price. A bureau of standards inspected weights and measures and the purity of goods. The obligation to unemployed and disabled workers and the families of soldiers was recognized; doles and pensions were provided, and grants were given the poorer citizens so that they could afford to participate in political and recreational activities. Public works programs enlisted many people in constructive service to the community. In general, it may be concluded that, although Athens preserved a fair balance between private and public enterprise, private economic interests were regarded as subservient to public-political ones.

Revolutionary Conflict. In addition to the frequent interstate wars with which the Greeks plagued themselves, civil conflicts within cities often occurred, involving oligarchical (the wealthy few) and democratic factions. In his *History,* Thucydides gave an objective analysis, one might say a clinical record, of one such revolutionary situation and the distortion of values that came in its train. (*See Reading No. 10.*)

Aristophanes. In Athens the conflict between classes was for the most part lacking in extreme brutality, but it was none the less spirited. The landed aristocrats, who had become a minority party by 510, continued during the following century to oppose the majority policies of economic, military, and imperial expansion. During the war they favored a restoration of peace, and many of them were frankly pro-Spartan. A moderate, by no means bitter exponent of the conservative point of view was Aristophanes (c. 450–c. 385). Primarily a comedian, using all the tricks of the trade to make people laugh— slapstick, personal abuse, verbal absurdities, fantasy and vulgarity—he was also a social satirist. Looking back wistfully to the "good old days," he held up to ridicule the radical democratic leaders and policies in the *Acharnians* and the *Knights* (*see Reading No. 11a*), the peoples' juries (*Wasps*), the exploitation of so-called "allies," the imperialistic ventures, the warmongers, informers and profiteers (*Birds*), and the new ideas in education, morals, literature and philosophy (*Clouds, Frogs*). Scientists, Sophists, and Euripides, apart from the political leaders Pericles and Cleon, were his favorite targets. The fact that his unpopular political views were year after year officially presented in the state theatre is a striking indication of two things: first that Aristophanes stated his unpopular ideas so brilliantly that people wanted to hear them; second, that Athens not only tolerated but welcomed the expression of minority opinions, even during the critical years of war.

Other Conservative Critics. Among other critics of the democracy was the anonymous "Old Oligarch" who wrote an ill-tempered, blistering attack on democratic policies and procedures, in which he claimed they favored only the working class, gave slaves too much liberty, exploited the "allies," and were economically and politically irresponsible. Xenophon (c. 430–c. 354), a country gentleman of wide interests but limited intellectual acumen, wrote a favorable account of the daily conversations of Socrates (*Memorabilia*), a pro-Spartan and moralistic history of Greece from 411 to 362 (*Hellenica*), an idealized picture of Persian royal education (*Cyropaedia*), an account of a mercenary expedition in Asia Minor in which he took part under Cyrus the Younger (*Anabasis*), and treatises on the Spartan government and the management of estates. All have a sturdy anti-democratic bias.

There was unquestionably some justification in the criticism by conservatives. Probably the Athenian assembly would have made wiser decisions if there had been some checks on the immediate will of the people; the democratic majority was inclined to follow irresponsible leaders when those leaders had magnetic personalities; the policy of imperial expansion had developed an arrogant attitude toward the "allies." But judged by two tests: the over-all achievements of democratic Athens and the range of interests, knowledge and happiness of the average citizen, it would seem that the balance sheet was decidedly in democracy's favor.

The Conscience vs. Authority. Pericles in his

Funeral Speech declared that individual and minority
rights were respected in Athens. But no society can
avoid some conflict between the authority of government and the conscience of individuals who refuse to
accept governmental decisions. In the *Antigone,* Sophocles presents one such situation in the early history
of Thebes, with obvious sympathy and respect for the
rebel. But although Antigone is noble in her defiance
of the king (*see Reading No. 11b*), Sophocles shows
that she is far from being a saint; the problem of the
conscience versus authority may be complicated by many
human factors. Antigone is devoted to her religious duty
and to her brother, whose body she buries in spite of
Creon's dictum that he is to lie unburied as a traitor;
but she is also stubborn, hates Creon as a man as well
as a ruler, scorns her sister, disregards her fiancé,
glories in martyrdom, and at the end indulges in self-
pity. Creon, on the other hand, is no villain; he wants
to preserve law and order and do well by his people;
but he, too, is stubborn, refuses to listen to his son's
tactful arguments, resents being opposed by a woman,
mistrusts the motives even of the priest, and finally col-
lapses under the emotional strain. It is a vivid example
of the complexity of such situations; and the implied
lesson is clear: such stubbornness of will can lead only
to disaster. Authority and the conscience must try to
work things out together and come to a reasonable
solution. It is a typically Athenian formula, based on
democratic principles of conciliation.

Women's Wrongs. Women represented one minority which did not receive fair treatment. There continued
from early times a prejudice against them, and a definite
philosophy developed regarding their inferiority. A
woman could own no property; she had no vote; it was
difficult for her to secure a divorce; her place was in the
home, not in public places. Xenophon voices the general
point of view when he listed the chief virtues of a
woman as "temperance, modesty, and teachableness."
In the *Eumenides,* Aeschylus had Athena herself voice
the prejudice; and Aristotle went so far as to state
categorically the astounding dogma that woman was by
nature inferior. In the later fifth century, however, signs

of reaction against the prejudice began to appear. All three dramatists, Aeschylus, Sophocles, and Euripides, pictured some women as superior to their men in intelligence as well as courage; and Euripides concentrated upon the injustices done women by men. In the *Medea* he described one woman's revenge, and uttered through her a strong indictment against the prevailing prejudice. (*See Reading No. 11c.*)

Aristophanes also took up the cause, partly because it offered good comedy, partly because he regarded women as at least more conservative than men, and partly, perhaps, because he genuinely sympathized with them. In the *Lysistrata* they are pictured as stopping the war that men foolishly started and more foolishly were unable to end; in the *Thesmophoriazusae* they criticize Euripides; and in the *Ecclesiazusae* they take over the government. (*See Reading No. 11d.*) Plato gave women for the first time their full rights. In his *Republic* he declared unequivocally that women should be treated on precisely the same basis as men, with the single exception of physical strength, in public as well as personal occupations and professions. (*See Reading No. 11e.*)

Slavery. Another minority consisted of the slave population. Although slavery as an institution was accepted without question (and Aristotle actually argued that it was justified), the living conditions of Athenian slaves were far better than those usually associated with the word "slavery." First of all, it should be noted that most of these slaves were war captives from the northeast frontier and were screened in accordance with their ability and experience so that they would do the sort of work which they could do best. Second, the jobs they had in many instances paralleled those of citizens, and inscriptions reveal some instances where slaves were foremen supervising citizens. It is true that the slaves assigned to the silver mines had a hard and short life; but those employed by the city on public works projects, police and clerical jobs, enjoyed working conditions and wages similar to those of citizens. Some of them saved enough money to buy their freedom, after which they could live on in the city as resident aliens. Laws pro-

tected slaves from bodily harm or unfair exploitation by
their private masters, who bought them from the city for
domestic or industrial work. They wore no distinctive
dress or insignia to show their status. It is significant that
there was no protest recorded against slavery as an institution, and there were no slave revolts in Athens.
The explanation is that slaves on the whole had economic
security and a fair measure of self-respect and happiness.
Many of them shared to a considerable extent in enjoying
the civilization which they helped to create. So, even in
the undefensible institution of slavery, Athens showed its
characteristic flexibility and liberality of attitude.

Plato's *Republic.* In his *Republic,* Plato proposed
a system of government and education which would,
he believed, remedy the inefficiency and injustice which
he deplored in existing governments, especially his own
Athens. To democracy's claims of equality and liberty he
replied that men are not equal and should not be treated
as if they were; and as for liberty, although he granted
in the *Laws* that people work better when they have a
sense of freedom, he believed that the extreme freedoms
of democracy lead to anarchy. What, then, is the positive
alternative? What is a genuinely just society? The search
led Plato to refuse to accept such answers as "Might is
Right" and "A Social Contract," and instead analyze the
psychological make-up of both an individual and a
community into three parts: appetite, unselfish spirit,
reason. The individual lives justly, he concluded, when
all three elements are healthy and work harmoniously
together, guided by reason. So in a community, justice
prevails when the classes chiefly dominated by these
various motives—the producing class by appetite, the
soldier-guardian class by unselfish spirit, the philosopher
rulers and educators by reason—are healthy in performing their function and work harmoniously together, led
by the philosopher-kings. Plato devoted most of his attention thereafter to the means of educating the ruling
class of "golden" men. He declared it the first duty of
society to give every child an equal opportunity to show
to what class his ability and aptitude entitled him. Most
children after their elementary education would go into
the acquisitive vocations, which Plato obviously dis-

liked. Those who demonstrated that they had the capacity to proceed further would continue their education until they were fitted to be soldier-guardians; then only the most gifted intellectually would be chosen to complete the training in mathematical and abstract thought which would qualify them for political and educational leadership.

Once men were assigned to their respective classes, they would continue there; it would be most unjust, for example, for a worker or businessman or a soldier to be a ruler. The great lower class would be permitted to own private property in moderation, but a communistic system, including family life, would prevail among the two upper classes, so as to offer no temptation for them to put private interests ahead of public ones. This system was not confined by Plato to men; he advocated the same education and opportunities for women.

In his ranking of governments Plato put a genuine aristocracy of brains and devotion to public service at the top. If, however, such an ideal system could be established, he was not optimistic enough about human nature to believe that it would endure; it would degenerate, he declared, into the successive stages of timocracy (rule by men seeking personal prestige), oligarchy (rule by the wealthy few), democracy (rule by the majority), and tyranny (rule by one "wild beast"). Men who sought prestige would in time not be satisfied with that; they would want property for themselves. When they had it, they would oppress the poor until finally the poor would revolt and establish a democracy. But then the people, unable to govern themselves, would fall into the grip of a dictator.

Plato has been criticized in modern times both as a fascist and as a communist. Insofar as he advocated the absolute control of government and education by a small minority, he might be considered a fascist. But his minority, it must be noted, was to consist of people of the highest intelligence, motivated by unselfish service; this can hardly be said of any fascist system. Insofar as he advocated the abolition of private property for two of his three classes, he might be regarded as a communist. But here again it must be noted that only the minority of rulers and military guardians were to live in such a fashion; the great majority of people, Plato declared, needed and should have private property. The claim might be made with some reason that Plato was a democrat, for he advocated a system of universal education to discover and develop the capacities of each child; he wanted women to have careers on the same basis as men; and he visualized a society whose aim would be the common welfare and in which every person would do the work and win the rewards that his abilities merited. All these are sound democratic principles. Yet in his lack of faith in the intelligence and honesty of ordinary men and his unwillingness to give them any share in the control of government and education he was profoundly anti-democratic. Perhaps, concluding that it is dangerous to use such labels, we should call him merely a Platonist. (*See Reading No. 12.*)

Aristotle's Politics. Less impatient with existing governments than Plato, and more concerned with classifying them than with blueprinting a Utopia, Aristotle was none the less an aristocrat by birth, training, and conviction. The governments which have developed he classified under three broad headings: rule by one person, by a few, or by the majority. Theoretically a wise and benevolent monarch would be the ideal ruler, but once unlimited power was in the hands of one man the tendency was for tyranny, the worst form of government, to result. Similarly with rule by a few: if the few are the ablest and most unselfish people, the government will be good; but a group in power is likewise apt to degenerate into a self-seeking oligarchy, which may be expected to lead to a revolt of the masses. Democracy, with certain constitutional checks and balances ("polity") is good; but when the majority gives way to its unbridled selfish interests, it is bad—not so bad as the others, for, as Plato had previously said, democracy is bound to be weaker in both its virtues and its injustice than more concentrated control.

Aristotle had more faith in the judgment of common men than Plato did. The collective judgment, he claimed, may in general be expected to be superior to that of any one person or group. Furthermore, people can be educated in public responsibility by holding office, deliberating about policies, and electing their officials. The chief practical obligation of government, Aristotle believed, was to guarantee law and order and avoid revolution. A democracy with certain constitutional checks is one effective means toward that end. Another is the existence of a large and powerful middle class; its spirit of moderation and conciliation will check the selfishness of the rich and the envy of the poor, and provide that the community "shall pass through life safely."

And the purpose of government, its final cause? Aristotle stated that in ringing terms. Its purpose is a moral one: to create for all of its members a good life, rich in intellectual and aesthetic activity, leading to happiness. Within the state many lesser associations will make their contribution to this end; but the state will unite them all into the supreme association which guarantees justice and makes living together the generous sharing of the best things which life can offer. (*See Reading No. 13.*) Aristotle's aristocratic bias reappears, however, in his limiting the finest experience to citizen men of the leisure class. Women and slaves he regarded as inferior by nature; and farmers, workers, and businessmen as engaging in inferior occupations.

— 8 —

THE GREAT AGE: FOREIGN
RELATIONS

Herodotus the Anthropologist. Herodotus (c. 484–425) played a dual role: he was the historian of the fateful conflict between East and West, when the Persian Empire invaded Greece and was repulsed at Marathon, Salamis, and Plataea (490–478), because, according to Herodotus' moral interpretation of history, Persia had the arrogant pride that inevitably leads to ruin; and in building up the background for these events he traveled widely in Asia Minor and Africa and reported on the customs of the people there, thus being the pioneer anthropologist.

The accounts he gives of foreign ways and beliefs are interesting and often amusing; he reports what he was told by men of authority and common folk, not vouching for its accuracy, but frankly enjoying it. Most significant is his attitude of curiosity and his complete lack of condescension or disapproval, race prejudice, or intolerance. His conclusion is simply that "custom is lord of all." (*See Reading No. 14a.*) The same generosity was shown by Athens in welcoming aliens and political refugees to the city. Until the Peloponnesian War frayed the nerves of the people of Athens, her attitude toward foreigners, Greeks or others, was one of hospitality without discrimination.

Defensive Alliances. Although relations between the Greek city-states and foreign countries were on the whole friendly, within Greece itself there were constant controversies, and the cities always found it difficult to join forces in the face of danger from abroad. Fortunately, when the greatest early threat of all appeared, a loose alliance of many cities was temporarily formed to oppose the invasion of Greece by the Persian Empire (490–478); and, led by the Spartan army and the Athenian navy, it succeeded in repulsing the invaders. After the final victory, scores of the Greek cities on the coast of Asia Minor and the islands of the Aegean wished to form a permanent defensive alliance to guarantee resistance against any such future invasion. Sparta was asked to assume the leadership; but, protected by her mountains and concerned chiefly with keeping her own slave population in subjection, Sparta shunned any such "entangling alliances." Athens, however, welcomed the opportunity to take part in this cooperative venture, partly because she too feared future aggression by Persia, partly because she was ambitious to become the leader of the Ionian Greek cities.

The sacred island of Delos was chosen as the headquarters of the League, which was therefore called the Delian League. According to its constitution every member had an equal vote on the Council, impartial law courts at Delos were to settle disputes arising between member cities, and there were a common treasury and a common military force. The annual budget assigned contributions on the basis of the wealth of the various members, and the funds were supposed to be used for the purpose of building and operating a navy and administering the other functions of the League.

Unfortunately, this promising venture in international cooperation soon became converted into an Athenian Empire. The underlying reason was the superior naval strength of Athens. Her superior power led to her controlling the votes of the smaller states in the Council; soon the treasury was moved to Athens, and Athenian courts supplanted those at Delos. So cooperation yielded to domination by one major power, which in turn eventually led in 431 to the Peloponnesian War.

Imperial Policies. Under the stress of war, self-interest dictated to Athens an intolerant and cruel code. Thucydides reports two situations in which Athens demonstrated the ruthless tactics of an empire at bay. One was in 428 when the wealthy and strategic city of Mitylene tried to withdraw from the so-called Delian League. Athens promptly blockaded the island and starved the people into submission; then the Assembly met to decide on a punishment for these "rebels." Should it be death for the ringleaders, or death for all the men and slavery for the women and children? The Assembly voted the latter, on the motion of Cleon, the majority leader. Luckily, this was reversed in a later meeting in favor of the more moderate policy, but even that policy was voted purely on grounds of expediency—that such extreme cruelty would be bad for Athens' reputation. And Cleon restated his case for imperial rule in no uncertain terms. (*See Reading No. 14b.*)

The Melian Episode. In 416 another episode occurred which reveals even more clearly the increasing brutality of Athens' foreign policy. The small neutral island of Melos, Athens decided, would be a useful base for naval operations, so she sent envoys to invite Melos to join the "League." The people of Melos realized that the choice was between death in battle or servile submission, but tried to argue for continuing their neutrality. Athens countered with an unabashed statement of the "might makes right" policy (*see Reading No. 14c*); and when the Melians chose to fight, subdued them, killing or enslaving the inhabitants, and settling Athenians on the land. Such was the attitude of arrogance bred by empire and war. How one Athenian was affected by such cruelty is seen in Euripides' tragedy, *The Trojan Women,* produced, significantly enough, shortly after the Melian episode. It is an unforgettable picture of the brutality unleashed by war among the victorious Greeks and the suffering of the innocent enemy women and children.

9

THE GREAT AGE: INDIVIDUAL
VALUES

Patron Divinity and Hero. The personal values prized by any culture may be seen in the characters, divine and human, that are worshipped or admired. In Athens the patron divinity was Athena, worshipped on the Acropolis as Athena Parthenos (the Virgin), Athena Promachos (the Warrior), and Athena Ergane (the Worker). As the Virgin goddess she was born, according to the ancient myth, from the very brain of Zeus and represented statesmanlike understanding of practical problems. As the Warrior she defended her favorite city. As the Worker she was the patron especially of women's weaving and embroidery, herself an expert craftsman. So in her holy person were combined three essential characteristics prized by the Athenians—practical intelligence, courage, and artistic skill. Their national hero was Theseus, according to legend the early king who freed the city from paying human tribute to the Cretan Minotaur. Prior to the fifth century he had been regarded chiefly as a blithe warrior, athlete, and lover, a more graceful and sensitive local version of Heracles, the universal Greek hero. But by the Great Age he had developed into the contemporary image of the city that revered him. It was now Athena who was said to have sponsored his expedition "to bring a just doom on the unrighteous," which he did with an intelligence equal to his valor. The dramatists pictured him as having been democratically minded, even though a king. Aeschylus wrote at least two, Sophocles three, and Euripides five plays in which he played an important role, always as a considerate and public-spirited ruler, working for important causes, and defending the weak and helpless. In Euripides' *Suppliant Women* he argues at length the advantages of democratic rule. "Inform me," he says in Sophocles' *Oedipus at Colonus;* "I must have full knowledge before I reach a decision. . . . I shall see to it that this state is stronger than any one man. You have come to a city that observes justice and does nothing except with proper legal sanction." As a friend of the suffering he welcomed Heracles, when that hero was in anguish over having murdered his children during a fit of madness, and received him in Athens with the most tender sympathy; and in his own grief over the death of his son Hippolytus he showed his full measure of compassion. His temple became a refuge for maltreated slaves; and he was generally considered the champion of the poor and helpless. So Theseus, not limited by the known facts of an actual life, had grown as Athens grew, re-created after her own heart, in her own best image of insight and kindness.

Education.   The aims and methods of Greek education differed widely in various places; in Sparta, for instance, education was almost exclusively military, in Athens the basis was broadly liberal. Athenian children were trained at home up to the age of seven, told stories from the exploits of the heroes of the past and Aesop's animal fables, and taught many games of skill. The rest of the girls' education was in domestic science at home. The boys went to school from seven to fourteen, where they had primary instruction in physical education and in "music," the latter including reading and memorizing poetry and reciting it to musical accompaniment, a combination of literature, speech, and music. Other courses included arithmetic and drawing. There was also instruction in personal and public ethics. After the age of fourteen only the wealthier boys could continue their education. From fourteen to eighteen they studied mathematics, rhetoric, and literature. From eighteen to twenty all young men were enrolled in military service, in the course of which many "saw the world" in the navy, or were stationed at various far-flung outposts of the empire. Following this period, the wealthy young men could have advanced instruction by enrolling for courses in rhetoric, public speaking, ethics, and the like, under the Sophists who came to Athens for protracted stays, or in schools like Plato's Academy. But all residents of the community shared in the adult education provided by the city: the musical, dramatic, athletic, and religious festivals, the public works programs employing leading architects, sculptors and painters, some contact with the intellectual leaders of Athens, and, for the citizens, a constant education in politics and the wide range of problems presented to Athenian voters and executives.

Athletics.   Physical education was not only regarded as one of the chief elements in formal education, it was also sponsored by cities for local festivals and for developing athletes to represent them at the great international games at Olympia, Delphi, Nemea, and the Isthmus of Corinth. Never again until modern times has the athlete been so encouraged and honored. As early as the heroic age there were well developed athletic meets, described in Book 23 of the *Iliad* and Book 8 of the *Odyssey,* including races, weight throwing, boxing, and wrestling. At the great international games, which increased in number and importance from the eighth century on, there were additional events, including the pancratium, an over-all contest in strength, skill, and endurance. Athletes who won at these meets were greeted with elaborate victory odes (Pindar was the poet laureate who commemorated the victories of scores of these athletes) and were lavishly entertained at public expense. But it was not only star athletes who received attention. In the cities there were many gymnasiums and athletic clubs, where instruction and facilities for enjoying the various sports were available. That a sound body was the most favorable environment for a sound mind was a generally accepted belief among the Greeks. Sports during the Great Age were primarily conducted on an amateur basis, and any great emphasis on specialization was deplored. Only in the later Hellenistic period did amateur athletics give way to professionalism, and watching contests become more important than taking part in them.

Classical Art.   In the art of this period many values

which appealed to Greeks of the Great Age were expressed. Whether it is a temple like the Parthenon, a bronze statue of Zeus hurling his thunderbolt, a vase painted by Polygnotus, a piece of furniture, or a mirror, there are certain characteristics which may be called "classical."

Negatively the term means that the abstract, grotesque, and exaggerated were avoided. Positively it means: (1) A healthy human norm. The human body provided the scale; temples were not gigantic, but were planned to please anthropomorphic divinities; sculpture and painting usually pictured healthy people in enjoyable activity. (2) A synthesis of design and naturalism. The geometric element was pronounced in over-all design and proportion, thus giving clean, firm, and logical structure, but it never went to the extreme of sheer abstraction; in sculpture and painting it was integrated with adequately naturalistic forms. (3) Refinement of detail. Once the essential structure had been established, the most loving care was given to refinement of detail. In buildings the relationships of the various elements were calculated most subtly, so that the effect is one, not of mechanical uniformity, but of flexibility and resilience. So with the sculpture: sensitive handling of line and modulations of mass give freshness and charm. (4) Serenity of mood. The combination of clarity of design and refinement of detail produces an effect of poise and dignity which is tremendously satisfying. Lacking sheer abstraction, realism, and nervously dramatic exuberance, this art's chief virtue lies in the logic of its structure, the refinement of its details, and its expression of human sanity and dignity. Even one of the humblest of the arts, that of the potter, illustrates this mood. In the middle of the fifth century the shapes of the vases had become streamlined without fussy detail; the scenes painted on them were generally of quiet subjects, in broad and monumental designs and free-flowing rhythm; amplitude and dignity replaced the pioneer nervous tension.

Art in this period was essentially a community affair. The great buildings and sculpture were city projects, enlisting the interest of the people and expressing their aspiration. The most ambitious project was Pericles' building program. From 450 to 420 no less than six major temples, the entrance hall to the Acropolis, the Hall of Mysteries at Eleusis, and a music auditorium were erected; and Hippodamus was brought from Miletus to plan the port of the Piraeus on a geometric basis. In their buildings the architects used both the Doric and Ionic styles, but modified them so as to combine grace and strength in a typically Athenian way. And to make them more worthy of the city, more capable (in Pericles' phrase) of cheering and delighting the Athenians as they saw them daily, sculptors and painters joined forces with architects and statesmen in a spirit of enthusiastic co-operation.

In both its architecture and sculpture the Parthenon may profitably be studied as an outstanding example of this classical art. The first impression it gives is one of noble simplicity and of structure based upon an austere geometry. But closer inspection reveals that the proportions were so subtly calculated and the refinements so delicately executed that the building has intimate charm as well as sober power. It avoids monotony by a complicated series of curved lines and planes. Its sculptural decoration was consistent with the architecture, having a similar amplitude and dignity of composition, with winning variety in the details. The pediments pictured the divine protection of the city: on the east end the birth of Athena was represented, on the west end the contest between Athena and Poseidon for the lordship of Athens. These groups were skillfully planned to fit within the triangular shape of the pediment, and the figures rose from the corners to the center in a fluent lateral rhythm, with drapery interweaving from the background outward to help build up the stalwart forms by casting shadows across them in the strong sunlight. The metopes, representing Greeks subduing Centaurs and Amazons, were composed in interesting horizontal, vertical, oblique, and circular patterns which provided effective secondary decoration; and the continuous frieze within the colonnade, recording the people of Athens coming to worship in the Panathenaic festival, was delightful in design as well as in narrative and pictorial interest. Here was art genuinely expressive of the clarity, strength, technical skill, and graciousness which were cherished by the people.

Patriotic Courage. Among the individual virtues most prized by the city-states, so proud of their independence, was patriotic courage. "Remember," Pericles had said, "that the secret of happiness is freedom, and freedom is created by courage." In many epitaphs over fallen soldiers, the cities of Greece in the fifth century praised their dead. (*See Reading No. 15a.*) Herodotus recounts the Athenian tradition in his story of Solon and Croesus (*see Reading No. 15b*) and his tribute to democracy. (*See Reading No. 15c.*) And the record of the most glorious of all their victories, that over the Persian armada at Salamis, was given eloquent tribute in the play by Aeschylus devoted to that triumph, the *Persians*. (*See Reading No. 15d.*)

The Moral Courage of Socrates. Another kind of courage was equally prized, as it always has been by free men: the courage of standing up for one's convictions. The most dramatic example of this courage was that shown by Socrates on three notable occasions. The first was when, as chairman for a day of the Council of 500, he defied an hysterical public demand for the mass trial and execution of generals who had failed to recover the bodies of several hundred soldiers killed in the sea battle of Arginusae (406). He claimed, quite properly, that such action would be unconstitutional. The second incident occurred during the short period following the defeat of Athens when the notorious anti-democratic government known as the Thirty was in power, thanks to Spartan backing. They tried to make Socrates share in their policy of persecution, but he bluntly refused. Finally, when he was on trial on charges of being a subversive influence, with death proposed as the penalty, he would not yield an inch or even try to be diplomatic; instead, he argued that his criticism of men and institutions was the best thing that could happen to Athens. (*See Reading No. 15e.*)

Why did Athens put a man like this to death? In defense of the majority of the jury who voted for his conviction it should be noted that nerves were frayed following a long and lost war, that Socrates had been critical of some democratic policies and procedures, that among his former followers were leaders of the anti-democratic forces in a blood-bath during their short stay in power at the end of the war (Socrates was considered "guilty by association"), and that most of the jurors who voted "guilty" doubtless expected that Socrates would propose exile as the alternative penalty. They simply wanted him out of the city; but when he defied them and refused to consider exile they voted the death penalty. It was one of the few instances of radical intolerance in the history of Athens. One must, however, bear in mind that Socrates had practiced his profession without interference for nearly fifty years prior to his being brought to trial.

The Life of Reason. Lovers of freedom, of diversity, of courage—we have seen Athenians of the Great Age as all of these. But perhaps the chief characteristic of this period is the high evaluation placed on the rational control of experience and the ability to solve problems by objective consideration and discussion. It appears in Pericles' Funeral Speech. It is the theme implied in many of the tragedies. The finest single statement of the faith is perhaps the chorus from Sophocles' *Antigone* in which the genius of man is praised. (*See Reading No. 16a.*) But it is recognized that the great skills acquired by man in mastering nature and fashioning communication and institutions can be used by him for self-destruction as well as for progress. The play, a conflict of stubborn wills, illustrates the point.

Destiny and Freedom. But of what value is reason if human life is in the control of the gods or of Destiny, as priests and earlier poets had declared? The three great dramatists of Athens tried to answer that question. Although Fate and the gods still remain in the traditional plots they used, their treatment of the characters indicates that men and women actually choose their destiny, and their own tragic errors bring about their doom. At the least, men have no sure way of knowing what decisions powers beyond them may have made (although those powers apparently dislike human excess and pride), so they must make their decisions on the basis of their own best judgment. Furthermore, those powers, apparently often at variance among themselves, fail to give men clear instructions as to what they should do, and often seem willing to let men make their own decisions. Sometimes a man's best judgment may seem to incur divine displeasure; but it may be argued, as Euripides does, that his moral sense is superior to that of the god. So much for the survival of divine intervention in the tragedies. But in most of the plays the sense of any ultimate determinism grows dim and largely or totally irrelevant; characters more and more disregard the existence of the gods or of Destiny in making their decisions; they rely upon their own experience and reasoned judgment in deciding what to do. Who will say that the conflict between Medea and Jason in Euripides' *Medea* or between Antigone and Creon in Sophocles' *Antigone* is more than a conflict of human wills? In Euripides' *Alcestis,* the wife of Admetus freely chose to sacrifice herself to save her husband's life when he was fated to die. Euripides' plays are often clinical studies of neurotic women, such as Phaedra and Electra, or of emotionally unbalanced men like the mad Heracles. Such instances could be multiplied at length. They indicate that the dramatists were concerned chiefly with probing into the consequences of human purposes in conflict, with the rational and fallacious judgments of men in shaping their destiny, with the failures and achievements of human freedom.

Finally, it should be noted that the tragic error of nearly every play is a pride of mind or emotional arrogance which makes the rational reconciliation of differences impossible. Thus, the ideal of the dramatists, like that of Pericles, would seem to be the man of sound judgment, eager to consider various points of view and come to a reasoned agreement with any honest opponent.

The Rational Recording of History. Thucydides in writing his *History of the Peloponnesian War* signally exemplified the Greek confidence in the method of reason. Although an Athenian and in all probability a moderate democrat in his political convictions, he made the most earnest effort to be objective in his description of events and his analysis of motives; one might say that he presented case studies of social disorder as objectively as

Hippocrates did his clinical records of individual diseases. He recorded the three stages by which Athens converted the Delian League into her Empire: first, the fear of Persia which she shared with her allies; then her pride in her increasing domination of the League in military, financial, legal, and cultural terms; finally, her brutal self-interest when her power was threatened. He reported with scrupulous accuracy the events of the war, such as the siege of Athens, the plague that smote the city, and the various naval engagements. One of his devices added drama to his account: his reporting, as well as he could recall them or find out about them, the actual speeches and debates of political leaders and diplomatic envoys. Thus, the discussions leading up to the war, the debate in the Athenian assembly regarding punishment for the "rebels" of Mitylene, and the attempt of Athenian diplomats to convince neutral Melos that it would be to her advantage to submit to Athens, all sound in our ears with the vividness of a contemporary recording. And the implicit lesson of his history—that too much power leads to arrogance, and that in turn to disaster—is traced with unerring skill and buttressed with an abundance of evidence, especially in the tragic debacle of the Athenian expedition against Syracuse. (*See Reading Nos. 9, 10, 14b,c.*)

The Socratic Method. To be reasonable—yes. But what is the process of reason? Now for the first time people began to study the working of the human mind. "The uncritical life," said Socrates, "is not worth a man's living." He devoted his life to the analytical study of the concepts men have, such as of freedom, piety, friendship, and justice, believing that if men try to define what those terms mean and to communicate the exact meanings to others, they will be on the road to living in terms, not of mere conjecture or habit, but of understanding. So he evolved a technique of cross-examination. When the first easy definition was given he would lead the person to see its shortcomings; then other definitions rephrased in view of the concrete particulars Socrates suggested would be tried out; finally, perhaps no satisfactory definition would be arrived at, but in the process two valuable experiences were gained: the complexity of the situation and the inadequacy of any easy solution appeared, and at least some phases of the truth had been discovered. (*See Reading No. 16b.*)

As far as conclusions were concerned, there was one that Socrates was strongly convinced was true: knowledge is goodness. He believed that all error is due to ignorance, and once a man knows what is right he invariably will do it. Such knowledge, however, must be defined; it is not knowledge of any particular skill, but rather the knowledge of human relationships which may be called insight or understanding; it is not being a "good" carpenter—or a "good" burglar—but a good man that Socrates had in mind. Now this doctrine may rest upon too optimistic a view of human nature; Socrates was living in a pre-Christian and pre-Freudian age, when the destructive urges of human beings were perhaps insufficiently realized. But it must be granted that within its limitations it is a sound theory. "He didn't know any better" is one of the genuine explanations of crime; and education is the basis of much of our penal reform as well as of positive ethical practices.

Plato's Rational Man.   Continuing Socrates' method of dialectic, Plato extended the study of concepts and of the nature of ideas. In the *Phaedrus* he compared a man to a chariot team, consisting of a powerful brute of a horse (appetite), a thoroughbred (unselfish spirit), and the charioteer (Reason). Only Reason can see the goal to be achieved and discipline the two horses to work together toward that goal. In his dialogues Plato demonstrated not only results of the reasoning process, but also case studies of the process itself; hypotheses were proposed, tested in terms of experience, modified or rejected, amplified, sharpened. And Plato believed that by this process one grows from knowledge of small areas to constantly more comprehensive ones, including interrelationships in laws and institutions, science and ethics, until, finally, one reaches a coordinated understanding of the universal good. (*See Reading No. 16c.*)

Plato's Theory of Art.   Among his analyses of concepts Plato included pioneer aesthetic criticism. He arrived at two conclusions: (1) art imitates nature; (2) art is to be evaluated chiefly in terms of its moral effect.

A work of art, he believed, imitates a physical object, hence is less real than its more substantial prototype; but since the physical object itself is less real than the concept which it imperfectly embodies, art is doubly removed from reality. Its technical excellence is to be judged in terms of the accuracy with which it copies the material world. As such it has importance in elementary education, training the senses of the young. But its chief importance, Plato concluded, lies in its molding sound moral character. Literature which inspires people to be brave, sober-minded, truthful, and magnanimous is the only kind that should be permitted. Music that is effeminate, plaintive, and convivial must be discarded, and only those harmonies retained which "represent the tones and accents of a courageous man acting with sobriety and moderation, the natural rhythms of a well-regulated and manly life." Similarly with the other arts: the philosopher-rulers will admit into their city only those artists who will "imitate the style of the virtuous man." (*See Reading No. 16c.*) Properly interpreted there is much to be said for both of Plato's points, although his conclusions are obviously inadequate; art is more than imitation of nature, "moral" requires careful definition, and censorship (even by philosophers) is a threat to the creative spirit. But regardless of their validity, they were useful in stimulating later study of the function of art in individual and social experience.

Aristotle's Virtuous Man. Less the poet and more the practical scientist than Plato, Aristotle made a rigorous analysis of the thinking process and a detailed series of precise definitions; he formulated the principles of formal logic and classified fallacies. Accepting as axiomatic that happiness is the goal of human life, he proceeded to study the essential quality of human happiness and ways of arriving at it. Happiness, he concluded, is an activity of the soul in accordance with virtue. Many virtues, such as courage, generosity, and high-mindedness, are found to lie in a mean between extremes. The period of life in which men naturally live in accordance with this principle is middle age. Thus much of the folk wisdom of the Greek people, favoring moderation, found philosophical justification in the conclusions of Aristotle.

Obviously any such summary as this cannot pretend to do justice to the extremely detailed analysis which Aristotle made of the various virtues. He distinguished in every category several types and degrees, refusing to be satisfied with facile generalizations. Courage, for example, he defined as a mean between fear and recklessness; but he proceeded to show how some things, such as disgrace, should be feared, and how spurious much so-called "courage" is. Virtues such as practical wisdom, primarily intellectual, can be learned; but others, like temperance, are moral and are cultivated by habit. In his down-to-earth way Aristotle concluded that more than rational activity and sound moral habits are needed; a fair measure of wealth is also necessary for happiness, and good birth, good looks, and joy in one's children play an important part. And a complete life must be reckoned with, for "as one swallow on a single fine day does not make the summer, so a single day or short period of delight does not make a man really happy." (*See Reading No. 16d.*)

Aristotle's Analysis of Tragedy.   Aristotle considered that the writers of tragedy were among the most effective teachers of virtue. By spectators sharing vicariously in the tragic error of a person capable of great experience and going through the sequence of events leading to his downfall, Aristotle believed that their feelings of pity and fear are aroused, and when they leave the theatre they have a better understanding of human experience. Analyzing the various elements in a play, he termed the plot by far most important, since it develops the theme of the error and its outcome; it may emphasize life as it is, as it appears to be, or as it ought to be; and it heightens its effect by such devices as suspense, irony, reversal of a normal situation, and a final recognition of the truth. Next in importance comes the skillful portrayal of the characters involved: the tragic hero or heroine must be neither a villain nor a saint, but essentially a person like us except for greater intellectual or emotional capacity. Next comes "rationalizing," the way in which characters try to justify their action to themselves and to others. Of lesser importance are the elements of poetic diction, music, and spectacle. The only dramatic unity which Aristotle insisted on was unity of action—that the plot should be logically constructed. And through the inevitable sequence of events in a great tragic play the purpose is accomplished of arousing pity for those who suffer, fear that we might make some such tragic error ourselves, and the final relief from emotional strain. (*See Reading No. 16d.*)

Other Tragic Values. There were, however, other values either ignored or inadequately treated by Aristotle in his technical analysis of tragedy. (Perhaps they were included in his discourses; what we have are little more than his lecture notes.) Among them should be mentioned the value of the chorus as an emotional reaction to the action of each episode, and to some extent a thoughtful interpretation of it, and the value of the messenger's speech describing the tragic climax, appealing to the spectator's imagination while sparing him the actual scene of horror. There was also the value of the dramatic festival itself, during which for three days the residents of Athens faced together some of the great problems of human decision, and doubtless, in the Athenian way, argued long after the productions were over what the dramatists had in mind and how right or wrong they were. And finally, although pity and fear are doubtless aroused by the plays, and the spectator may be purged of such emotions, the ultimate value of tragedy was hardly more than suggested by Aristotle: the broadening and deepening of experience by seeing people of great emotional and intellectual capacity face situations more terrible than they can overcome, however resourceful and brave they may be. This inspires more than pity and fear; it arouses admiration and a fellow-feeling for men and women of heroic stature, even when they err and suffer; and it leads to more generous and sensitive insight. The ultimate value of the life of tragedy, as John Masefield once said, is that through it we become better able to understand and endure the tragedy of life. (*See Reading No. 17.*)

Hybris and Sophrosyne. In appraising the scale of values of the Great Age, what shall we conclude were the chief attitudes which the Greeks thought should be avoided and be cultivated?

There can be little question that the chief sin was considered to be *hybris,* "arrogant pride." Too much of any material thing, especially money and power, they thought, is apt to lead to such pride, which distorts a man's clear judgment, blinds him to plain facts, and ultimately brings him to disaster. "Pride comes before a fall." The epic legends had already pointed up the lesson; in the *Iliad,* Agamemnon's supreme power and Achilles' pre-eminence as a fighter made them so proud that they forgot their duty to the common cause of their people; the result was disaster to themselves as well as the men who depended on them. A leading theme in the *Odyssey* was the insolence of the suitors for Penelope's hand; because of their arrogance they were an easy prey for the cool-headed Odysseus when he returned home. The same moral was drawn from the defeat of Persia at Marathon and Salamis. Herodotus and Aeschylus agreed on the explanation: it was not that the Persians were as a people inferior to the Greeks, it was the *hybris* of the invader; in Aeschylus' words, "Pride, after it blossoms, produces fruit of doom and a harvest of tears." *Hybris* is the tragic flaw in many of the characters in Greek drama. The revolutions in Greek cities, deplored by Thucydides, were caused, he declared, "by greed, ambition, and the love of power." Plato considered the acquisitive motive so dangerous that he prescribed moderation as the chief virtue to be cultivated by businessmen and workers, and permitted his ruling class no private property whatever. Aristotle regarded the acquisition of great wealth or power as a primary evil. Finally, Athenians after 400 could hardly fail to realize that their own imperial power had led to arrogance that blinded their judgment and brought about their defeat.

Opposed to *hybris* was the positive virtue which the Greeks called *sophrosyne,* "intelligence which keeps people secure," or "saving sense." The word has often been translated as "prudence," "sobriety," or "temperance," but these are much too negative words. The Greeks recognized that emotions must be kept vigorous and alert, but that an even stronger intellectual faculty must guide them. Countless references might be cited to the way in which this attitude was praised during the Great Age.

It was emphasized constantly in the tragic dramas. Pericles paid tribute to it in his Funeral Speech. In one of the debates reported by Thucydides it is underscored: "There is no disgrace in showing reasonable self-control, for by it we avoid insolent prosperity and do not surrender to adversity." Socrates, in the only prayer of his which has been preserved, asked to have only as many possessions as a man with saving intelligence could manage. The great pity is that, understanding and esteeming this attitude as they did, the Greeks of the fifth century were not able to apply it more effectively in their interstate relations and thus avoid their suicidal wars.

10

THE DISPERSION: THE SETTING

Macedonian Supremacy. The battle of Chaeronea in 338 sealed the doom of the free cities of Greece. Previously, various ones had dominated others for short periods of time; now all were destined to fall under the control of Macedon, and their political autonomy was to be virtually at an end.

The reasons for this loss of freedom deserve careful study, as every loss of freedom does. One reason was the military genius and political shrewdness of Philip of Macedon. Pioneering in the devices later used by many dictators, he first created a superb fighting force, proud of its tactical skill and fanatically loyal to him. Then he used this army to conquer small neighboring states, including a gold-mining area which provided useful revenues for his military and diplomatic ventures. His next step was to weaken in every possible way the will to resist in the more important states to the south, especially Athens and Thebes. He was friendly to the businessmen ("You can do business with Philip"); he assured the war-weary political leaders that he had no further aggressive designs; he craftily suggested the possibility of eventually conquering their ancient enemy, Persia; and to crown it all he drew on his copious treasury for outright bribes when that method was likely to be effective.

An equally important reason was the susceptibility of the free states to such strategy. They had so exhausted themselves by constant wars, and individualism had so far supplanted the civic responsibility of the earlier days, that the morale for resistance was at a low ebb. Furthermore, Philip's ability was so obvious and his claims

seemed so praiseworthy that many patriotic citizens genuinely believed that in his leadership lay their best hope
for Greek unity, progress, and peace.

So it is not surprising that when Philip struck de-
cisively the resistance at last organized, but much too
little and too late, was ineffective. After his victory at
Chaeronea, Philip adopted a fairly lenient policy toward
the Greek cities; but Macedonian supremacy was soon
made most explicit by Alexander the Great.

As Alexander proceeded to extend his conquests to
distant, non-Greek lands, he was an ardent cultural mis-
sionary as well as a military victor. The instruction which
he had received in his teens from Aristotle had developed
in him intellectual interests which bore fruit in the
colonies of Greeks which he established as his armies
moved eastward toward India; and the influence of these
Greek institutions, ideas, and art lingered and spread
there long after Alexander's death spelled the disappear-
ance of Greek military and political control.

The Hellenistic Age.   The period from the death of
Alexander the Great (323) to the conquest of Greece
by Rome, some 200 years later, is known as the Hellenistic Age. Alexander's empire was split into three parts,
with centers in Macedonia, Asia Minor, and Egypt.
Along with the loss of political independence there were
other distinctive characteristics of the Hellenistic period.
Elements of Greek culture were extended to many areas
where they had either previously not penetrated or had
not been so influential. A new emphasis was put on
private enterprise, shown in increasing specialization;
notably at Alexandria, a great university center developed specialized research in many fields, literary as
well as scientific. The comedy of manners of Menander
(342–291) supplanted the comedy based on community
problems of the Great Age, and tragedy gave way to
romantic verse and fiction. There was a greater concern
with practical science. Many cults arose, religious, philosophical, and aesthetic; and there was a growth of skepticism and a sense of futility. Men were losing their confidence in the rational control of themselves and of
society.

The Roman Conquest.   This process was continued

after the conquest of Greece by Rome. Henceforth, Greek culture followed the Roman legions as it had previously followed Alexander's army; for although Rome achieved a military victory over Greece, Greece was the cultural conqueror of Rome. Wealthy Romans sent their sons to Athens for their liberal education; Greek teachers and artists were in demand in Italy; and Greek literature and art, philosophy and religion, were adopted by the Romans. The seeds from the ancient tree of Greece were scattered to the four winds, to sprout to new life all over the world. So it is not accurate to call the Hellenistic culture "decadent"; it was a process, not of dying, but of dispersion, which stimulated new growth wherever it went.

— 11 —

THE DISPERSION: MAN, NATURE, AND GOD

The Stoics. Among the popular philosophies which sought to compensate for the loss of political liberty and give people self-confidence and courage in the face of adversity, the chief one was Stoicism. It derived many of its tenets from the principles of the earlier idealistic philosophers. The pioneer Stoic (the name comes from the covered porch —*stoa*— in which he taught) was Zeno of Athens (c. 270). Its interpretation of the world is seen in the eloquent *Hymn to Zeus* by Cleanthes (331–232) (*see Reading No. 18a*), and in the *Discourses* and *Manual* of Epictetus (c. 80 A.D.) a slave at the court of Nero. (*See Reading No. 18b.*) According to their philosophy, the world is controlled by omnipotent and perfect Universal Reason. Men therefore live in a morally planned universe, in which they have their role to play, and a noble role, since they have within themselves part of the divine element; their role is to recognize and live in accordance with this guiding principle of Nature. In their attempt to define the principle in physical as well as moral terms, the Stoics contrived some bizarre explanations of cyclical cosmic conflagrations; but their real concern was not with physical but with moral interpretations of the world.

In their moral interpretation they accepted the fact that evil exists. How can that be, if an omnipotent and utterly virtuous Reason governs the world? Their explanation (which was to be repeated in many later times by theologians) was that the perfect plan includes giving men some freedom of choice; only by exercising such freedom can moral strength be attained. So men may live reasonably, but they may choose instead to indulge in the spurious satisfactions of wealth, prestige, and sensual pleasure. Such choice is error; and the error is evil. But even that evil is part of a perfect universal design, which the Stoics praised with religious fervor.

Epicurus. The most important rival of Stoicism as a popular philosophy was Epicureanism, founded by Epicurus (341–270), who spent most of his life in Athens at his school, which was called the Garden. Epicurus adopted the atomic theory of Leucippus and Democritus. He declared that nothing exists except atoms moving in empty space; a property of the atoms is an occasional swerve, which results in new and unpredictable patterns. So the universe cannot be regarded as planned or even mechanistically regular; the element of luck plays an important part in it. The human mind, he said, is made up of very fine atoms, which are dispersed when death occurs. So there is no personal immortality. As for the gods, according to Epicurus they exist as combinations of very fine atoms, but they have their own far-off world where they enjoy themselves, and have no concern whatever with human affairs. (*See Reading No. 19.*) Sense perception is the only basis of knowledge; error comes through reason rather than through the senses. Sense perception is true because "effluences" shed from material objects actually enter our senses and form correct images there.

Skeptics. To an increasing number of critical men even the consolations offered by Stoics and Epicureans seemed self-deception; they found their chief satisfaction in skepticism. The lead in this attitude was taken by the Cynic (a "dog's life") philosopher Diogenes (c. 400–325) in Athens, noted for the pithy sarcasm with which he pilloried pretention and superstition. (*See Reading No. 20a.*) According to his positive philosophy, happiness is to be gained by satisfying natural needs in the simplest way, thereby attaining serene self-sufficiency. A much more detailed and devastating criticism of popular beliefs regarding the gods and of many aspects of human pretention was made by Lucian (c. 160 A.D.) a Syrian teacher of rhetoric, who wrote *Dialogues of the*

Gods and *The Gods in Council,* showing their all-too-human attributes, the *Sale of Creeds* and various other debunking essays. (*See Reading No. 20b.*) Among the professional philosophers in Athens a group of Skeptics went to the ultimate point of declaring that nothing can be known. Arcesilaus (c. 315–240) developed this theory in refutation of the Stoics' dogmatic assertion of the claims of reason. Another group, unable to accept the religious myths as objectively true, but trying to salvage something of value from the fading Olympian religion, interpreted the gods as simply glorified heroes, to be regarded as symbols of human qualities. This interpretation was first made by the Sicilian philosopher Euhemerus in the fourth century, and the theory, which was to have considerable subsequent acceptance (including a revival of it by the Church Fathers in the Middle Ages) was known as Euhemerism.

Science.   In the field of science, this was a period of creative achievement; specialization paid high dividends. Among the scientists interest had shifted from theories about the ultimate nature of the world—theories which seemed to have reached a dead end—to the exact description of nature and of means of controlling it for practical purposes. Euclid (c. 300) in his school in Alexandria formulated with beautiful clarity and precision axioms and propositions of geometry which laid the foundations for further research in mathematics, astronomy, and engineering. He also was a pioneer in geometric optics. (*See Reading No. 21a.*) Aristarchus of Samos (c. 310–230) arrived at the heliocentric theory, and described the rotation of the earth around its own axis. Eratosthenes of Cyrene (c. 275–194), head of the Library at Alexandria, figured out the circumference of the earth close to the actual figure, and calculated the size and distance of the sun and moon; he was also the first systematic physical and ethnological geographer. But the greatest scientific mind in the Hellenistic period, and for that matter one of the greatest in history, was Archimedes (c. 287–212) of Syracuse. Among many mathematical formulations which he made (including operations of the type of the integral calculus), the most important were in solid geometry and hydrostatics. (*See*

Reading No. 21b.) He invented the water screw, discovered the principle of moving a great weight by a small force, and by an arithmetical process discovered the upper and lower limits to π (3 1/7 and 3 10/71).

— 12 —

THE DISPERSION: MAN
AND SOCIETY

Stoics and Epicureans. In this time of political apathy and of flourishing specialization and individualism, community obligations of the earlier period seemed far from important to most people; the sense of public enterprise was fading out of the picture. Of the two great popular philosophies, Epicureanism frankly dismissed the matter with a shrug; all that shall concern us, it said, is individual happiness, and that is to be gained by ridding oneself of all fear and by choosing for oneself the qualitatively best and most enduring pleasures. Political and social ambition are to be shunned as deterents to happiness. Incidentally, in Epicurus' school for the first time women were admitted as members.

The Stoics, on the other hand, although they had somewhat the same aim as the Epicureans—the achievement of a basic serenity and self-sufficiency—projected their notion of a divine plan governing the universe to human society. Since all men share in Universal Reason, they are therefore brothers, they are fellow-citizens in the commonwealth of the world, and have a duty to play that part well. But in practice no such obligations could be allowed to disturb one's serenity of mind; no outward circumstance was regarded as worth worrying about. So even the Stoic's very real sense of duty and community responsibility was subservient to what he called his individual moral freedom; and he could not be counted on to wage a very determined battle against injustice when he believed that no external circumstance was really important. (*See Reading Nos. 18 and 19.*)

THE DISPERSION: FOREIGN RELATIONS

The Futile Opposition to Dictatorship. The period between the collapse of the Athenian Empire and the conquest of Greece by Macedon was politically a dreary one, of temporary hegemony first by Sparta and then by Thebes, and of shifting patterns of alliance. Athens occasionally tried to unite various Greek states into a coalition; but the Greek people were war-weary and the prevailing mood was one of private, not public, enterprise. Finally, however, facing the greatest threat since the Persian invasion, the independent city-states had to make the fateful decision whether to accept the rule of Philip of Macedon or attempt resistance. Two parties developed in Athens, one for appeasement, the other for resistance. The resistance movement was led by Demosthenes (384–322), who used his genius as a public speaker to urge Athens and the other free states of Greece to oppose Philip, calling him a tyrant who would reduce them to slavery. Opposing him were various groups; some refused to take Philip's designs seriously, others thought their business interests would be as successful with Philip as ruler as under a democratic regime, and many patriotic citizens, including some of the leading educators and politicians, were convinced that the day of the city-state was past, and Athens might better come to as advantageous terms as possible with a general as powerful and able as Philip, thus becoming part of a united Greece at peace, able to defend itself against any aggressor, and even take the initiative against Persia.

Demosthenes in his *Philippics* presented the case effectively against Philip and Philip's supporters. Recognizing the ability and military power of Philip and the shortcomings of the Athenian democracy, he, nevertheless, claimed that the Athenian principles of government and character were vastly superior to those of Philip, and he urged the Athenians to strengthen their armed forces, enter into effective alliances with other free states, go to the assistance of cities attacked by Philip, and, above all, revive the patriotic spirit of the earlier days. His fervent sincerity and oratorical skill finally moved Athens to action, but what she did was too little and too late. Perhaps Demosthenes' opponents were right in claiming that he was advocating a cause bound to be lost, that there was no future for independent small states, and that unification of the Greek world under a powerful ruler was desirable as well as inevitable. Obviously, Demosthenes overestimated the resources, material and spiritual, of Athens, and exaggerated the malignity of Philip, who in fact had great respect for Athenian culture. Perhaps a really effective alliance of Greek states was impossible. Yet, in leading his resistance Demosthenes was true to the finest Greek traditions: those of self-respecting freedom and of political responsibility. And after the city-states had fallen under dictatorial control, even though their traditional culture was extended to distant lands by Alexander the Great, the spirit which had created that culture was, as Demosthenes foretold, incurably wounded. (*See Reading No. 22.*)

Federal Union. It is apparent that as the outstanding virtue of the Greeks was their love of freedom, their outstanding weakness was the inability of the city-states to engage in constructive cooperation. There were, however, several defensive alliances, and a few attempts at federal union. The most promising was the Delian League, until Athens converted it into her Empire. Among other federations the most ably organized and directed was the Achaean League, an association of cities in southern Greece. Its double aim was to guarantee its members local autonomy and security from external aggression. To this end a League army, courts, and currency were adopted, and common policies were decided

by a Council which included representatives elected annually from all the member cities. A chief executive
officer was also elected annually. The ablest leader of the
League was General Aratus (271–213), democratic king
of Sicyon, but even his political skill was unable to make
the union effective when it came face to face with the
vastly superior military power of Macedon. The historian
of the League, Polybius (210–128), although he later
served as a Roman official and approved of Roman rule,
paid sincere tribute to this valiant attempt to make interstate cooperation a reality. The fact that such a federal
union succeeded as much and as long as it did is a
tribute to the Greek mind. (*See Reading No. 23.*)

— 14 —

THE DISPERSION: INDIVIDUAL
VALUES

Hellenistic Art. In the art of this period the values cherished by people in the sophisticated urban centers are very clearly indicated. The previous community sponsorship gave way largely to art regarded as a means for personal display and a source of satisfaction to the individual collector. Stylistically it mirrored the specialization, the eclectic variety, and the tendency toward exaggeration of the time.

When wealthy cities like Pergamon and Miletus erected civic centers it was on a spectacular scale, with buildings of various styles grouped for an overwhelming effect of great stairways, forests of columns, and pretentious sculptural decoration. The severe Doric style went out of fashion; the Ionic became more intricate in its details, though less subtly carved; and the florid Corinthian style came into the favor which it was to enjoy in the later history of Europe. But the chief change was in the attention given to luxurious private homes. In earlier times even the houses of wealthy men had been quite modest, but now architects spent much of their effort on devising comforts and displays for such homes.

In sculpture the three tendencies which began in the late fourth century: realism, romantic impressionism, and dramatic exaggeration, were further developed by sculptors who had learned how to use every technical device to achieve the effects they desired. Some of them studied and pictured anatomy with scientific accuracy; others noted the most delicate transitions of the play of light and shade across lovely bodies, and recorded evanescent and transitory charm; others pictured scenes of impetuous violence, as in the conflict of gods and giants on the Great Altar of Zeus at Pergamon and the group influenced by it, the famous Laocoön. But regardless of subject or technique, the clarity of design and serenity of mood of the earlier sculpture were usually regarded as outmoded. And most of the sculpture was now commissioned by wealthy patrons for their personal enjoyment instead of by cities for public projects. The previous wholehearted cooperation between the artist and his community had become converted into a pattern of private patronage.

Vases showed a similar evolution. The centers of pottery manufacture, now in Southern Italy, produced ware which emphasized bizarre ornamentation and casually complex paintings instead of good basic design in the shapes and illustrations.

Refuge in Philosophy and Religion.   The Hellenistic age was an age of the individual, but the individual without the political opportunity and responsibility that were formerly so dear to him, and without much faith in the traditional religion. Where, then, were assurance and happiness to be found? To this question Epicureanism and Stoicism, the two great philosophies, had answers which gave perplexed and frustrated people some measure of emotional security and peace of mind.

The Epicurean formula was this: first, get rid of fear, especially fear of the gods and of death, since neither concern men; the gods pay no attention to them, and there is no life after death to worry about. The next step is to reduce wants to those that can be readily satisfied, and to avoid all circumstances which might cause mental distress. Positively one should seek whatever pleasure of high quality and long duration chance permits one to have. In this way the individual will attain the serenity of mind and satisfaction of the senses which constitute true happiness.

The Stoics also sought freedom from fear; but they found it by having faith in Divine Providence and by ridding themselves of dependence on anything except that Providence and their own moral will. They recognized that there are many calamities which afflict mankind and which a brave man cannot seek to escape; but he can endure them, even rejoice in rising superior to them, if he refuses to be affected by anything external to himself. And what is external? His property, his family and friends, his reputation, his health, even his life, are in the power of other people; if he depends on such things he is bound to be miserable. Only his own mind and moral will are in his own control. By exercising them he not only can overcome every circumstance, but also can feel the supreme happiness of being part of Universal Reason. So, by a route other than the Epicurean one, the Stoic also arrived at the goal of self-sufficiency and freedom from fear. It was a more rugged route, and along it the Stoic did not hesitate to engage with difficulties and dangers that the Epicurean blandly avoided; but both found in their philosophy a similar assurance of some value in living. (*See Readings Nos. 18 and 19.*) For less philosophically minded people there was widespread refuge in religious cults of the mystery type, some imported from Asia Minor, and in reliance upon astrology and magical rites.

Refuge in Sentiment. However, there were other avenues of escape from the perplexing dilemmas of life. One was offered by poets, in voicing the enjoyments of nature, friendship, and love. In the *Greek Anthology* there are hundred of little poems, some of the valentine type, some literary *tours de force*, some tender and wistful, on those themes. (*See Reading No. 24c.*) The first such anthology was published by the poet Meleager about 90 B.C. In it he included more than one hundred of his own epigrams and presented it to his sweetheart, Heliodora, ascribing to the various poets characteristic flowers (hence the name "Anthology," "A Collection of Flowers"). Of Sappho, for instance, there were only a few, he said, but "every one was a rose." In later periods much larger collections of such Greek poems were made, covering a wide range of subjects, in Byzantium in the sixth, tenth, and fourteenth centuries A.D. Among the ablest of the Alexandrian poets was Callimachus (c. 305–c. 240), who held a post in the famous Library of Alexandria.

In periods of urban sophistication there has often de-

veloped nostalgia for the healthy physical life and serenity of mind presumably found in the country. Such
was the emotional refuge that Vergil provided for Rome,
Robert Burns for Edinburgh, and Robert Frost for
Boston. In Alexandria, the Sicilian poet Theocritus (c.
270) brought this back-to-nature freshness to the jaded
senses of urban society. He developed in his *Idylls* the
pastoral form of poetry, wherein shepherds and goatherds, resting in a spot of shade in a Sicilian landscape
drenched in sunshine, vied with each other in various
sorts of songs, including the laments which were to
furnish a pattern for such English poems as Milton's
Lycidas and Shelley's *Adonais*. He also did a series of
dramatic monologues: a love-sick girl performs a primitive hexing ritual by moonlight in a frantic effort to make
her apathetic lover return; two Syracusan women gossip
freely and frankly as they go together to the festival of
Adonis at Ptolemy's palace. There is a genial humor in
many of his poems, notably two in which the ugly Cyclops, Polyphemus, is pictured naïvely in love with Gala-
tea, a friskily teasing sea-nymph. Tender feeling charac-
terizes such *Idylls* as the one telling how the nymphs of
a spring fell in love with the lad Hylas and dragged him
down to his death, and the tribute which the reaper
Bucaeus sang to his sweetheart. (*See Reading Nos.
24a, b.*) Theocritus' followers, Bion and Moschus, treated
similar themes in a more florid and sentimental fashion;
but in Theocritus' poems there is always, in addition to
romantic charm, a sturdy vigor representative of the
countryside he loved so well, providing a tonic needed
by restless and distracted people in the Hellenistic cities.

Refuge in Satire. As is usually true in times of
depression and "failure of nerve," spotting other people's
faults gave satisfaction to many authors and their public.
As early as the fourth century, Theophrastus (c. 370–
c. 285) had in his *Characters* pictured with devastating
precision certain types of human pests, such as the boor,
the busybody, and the suspicious man. (*See Reading No.
25a.*) Lucian satirized mercilessly both gods and men.
Epigrams critical of various professions became popular;
the foibles of doctors, lawyers, teachers, and athletes

were pinpointed in caustic phrases. (*See Reading No. 25b.*)

Refuge in Pessimism. Finally, in this time of emotional and intellectual frustration, the ultimate cult arose: that of futility, the *fin-de-siècle* weariness with life itself which continued in the survival of Greek culture in Byzantium. The *Greek Anthology* gives in hundreds of beautifully turned epigrams the sense that life has no meaning; there is no joy in the present and no hope for the future. (*See Reading No. 25c.*) So did some Greeks write for their culture an undeserved epitaph; for having lived a long and useful life in its original environment, it was destined to live on, in far-off lands, woven into the stuff of later men's lives.

Why the Decline? The reasons for the decline of creative Greek culture have long since been implicit in this account, but perhaps a final summary may be useful. The complex situation defies any simple explanation; as many factors contribute to the creation of a culture, so do many account for its weakening vitality. The theory has been advanced that civilizations, like individuals, by a kind of natural process have periods of youth, maturity, old age, and death; but there are more plausible explanations than this. Certainly the loss of political liberty played a large part. Overspecialization led to less social unity and drive. The partial dependence on slave labor was responsible for lack of initiative with regard to technological and industrial experimentation. Human resources had been depleted by many wars. Moral standards had declined as civic responsibility and religious faith lessened. But certainly one of the chief reasons was the shattering of morale as individuals faced the complexities of urban living and a range of new knowledge so vast that its integration into a coherent and satisfactory philosophy of life seemed well-nigh impossible. In the face of this situation people were tempted to retreat from the attempt to understand and rationally control their lives. They found it far easier, as E. R. Dodds has said, to take "unconscious flight from the heavy burdens of individual choice which an open society lays upon its members" and cast their intellectual and emotional burdens on some absolute ruler, some priest, or some other leader who was willing or eager to accept the responsibility—and the power. Whatever the intricate web of causation, the civilization was tired. Escapism became the order of the day: refuge was sought in one's home, one's profession, social clubs, artistic circles, mystical cults, or in sheer apathy or despair.

But the final word is not one of despair. For the ideas created by the Greek mind at its best have continued ever since to stimulate the thinking of men and their confidence in the power and beauty of human reason.

Part II

SELECTED READINGS FROM GREEK BOOKS

— Reading No. 1 —

TRADITIONAL RELIGION

About 750[1] the farmer-poet Hesiod recorded traditional accounts of the creation and evolution of divine powers. In Homer's Odyssey *the Olympian gods are pictured as directing human affairs, and when Odysseus talks with Achilles in the realm of Hades, Achilles expresses the generally accepted view of the after-life. Release from present suffering and a happy immortality were promised those initiated into the mystery cult of Dionysus, praised by his followers in Euripides'* Bacchae.

✓   ✓   ✓

a. HESIOD: *Theogony*

In the beginning was Chaos, and next broad-bosomed Earth. From Chaos came Erebus and black Night, and of Night and Erebus were born Air and Day. And Earth bore the starry Heaven to cover her and become the home of the blessed gods. She also bore the unharvested sea. Later to Earth and Heaven was born Cronos (father of Zeus), the cunning youngest and most fearful of her brood.

---

b. HESIOD: *Works and Days*

The immortal gods are close to men and observe those who with unjust judgments grind their fellowmen down, heedless of the gods' wrath. For countless immortals walk upon the bounteous earth and note men's cruel deeds

[1] All dates are B.C. unless otherwise specified.

and judgments. And Justice, Zeus' daughter, glorious and revered among the Olympian gods, also keeps watch.

———————

c. HOMER: *Odyssey* I

After the war at Troy all the other heroes who had escaped death in battle or at sea returned home. But Odysseus had not returned, although he was longing for his home and his wife. And even when the time came that had been set by the gods for his return to Ithaca, he still was not over his troubles. All the gods except Poseidon felt sorry for him, but the lord of the sea never ceased being violently angry against Odysseus.

Now the rest of the gods (Poseidon was away visiting the Ethiopians) were gathered in the palace of Olympian Zeus, where the father of gods and men began to address them. Thinking of the hero Aegisthus, whom Agamemnon's son Orestes had killed, he said, "See how mortals blame the gods, saying their troubles come from us, when actually their own folly brings worse troubles on them than fate ever planned. Aegisthus over-reached himself when he became the lover of Agamemnon's wife and killed Agamemnon on the day of his return home from Troy. Aegisthus was well aware of the fact that he would die for it, for we had sent Hermes to warn him. 'Vengeance will come,' Hermes said, 'from Orestes when he grows up and longs to return to his own country!' But Hermes' warning did not restrain Aegisthus, and now he has paid the penalty."

Then gleaming-eyed Athena said, "Father, lord of lords, it was right that Aegisthus died. May every one die who acts as he did. But I am heartbroken as I think of Odysseus, so resourceful yet so unlucky. For a long time he has endured all sorts of misfortunes, exiled from kith and kin, on a wave-wracked island, Calypso's home. She keeps the poor man from going on his way, trying to beguile him with clever talk so that he will forget Ithaca. But Odysseus wishes only to see the smoke rising from his own home. O Ruler of Olympus, I am amazed that you care nothing about him. Weren't you satisfied with the sacrifices he made to you on the plain of Troy?"

Cloud-gatherer Zeus answered her, "My child, what a

way to talk! How could I forget noble Odysseus, who surpasses other men in insight as well as in offerings to the gods? It is Poseidon who hates him, because Odysseus blinded Poseidon's son, the Cyclops Polyphemus. Ever since that happened Poseidon has prevented Odysseus from returning to his ancestral home. But come now, let us all plan for his return. Poseidon will eventually get over his anger, he cannot oppose the other gods all by himself."

Then Athena said, "Father, lord of lords, if the blessed gods really wish Odysseus to return home, let us call Hermes and promptly send him to Calypso's island, to tell the fair-haired nymph of our fixed purpose to set long-suffering Odysseus on his way home. As for myself, I shall go to Ithaca to arouse his son and encourage him to speak boldly to all those suitors for his mother's hand. And I shall send him to sandy Pylos and Sparta, to ask those he meets for news of his father."

---

d. HOMER: *Odyssey* XI

Next came the ghost of Achilles. He recognized me, and wept. "Noble son of Laertes, ingenious Odysseus," he said, "why do you plan still crazier adventures? How could you think of coming down here to Hades, where only ghosts dwell, the mere shadows of men whom life wore out?"

I answered, "Achilles, mightiest of the Achaean warriors, I came to learn from the seer Tiresias how to get back to rocky Ithaca. So long I have been away, with misfortune always plaguing me. But you, Achilles, I consider the happiest man who has been or ever will be. While you were still alive we all honored you as if you were a god, and now in Hades' realm you are a prince among the dead. To you, Achilles, death can be no disaster."

To that he replied, "Don't talk lightly to me of death, noble Odysseus. I had rather work on earth as a hired hand for a poverty-stricken farmer than be king of all the ghosts down here."

---

e. EURIPIDES: *Bacchae*

PRIEST. You deride this new god, O king, but I cannot find words to describe his greatness. For there are two chief powers among men. One is Demeter, the Earth, by whatever name you want to call her; she nourishes mankind with dry food. The other is Dionysus, who discovered the flowing vine and gave it to men to end their long-suffered grief and bring the sleep which lets them forget their cares.

―――――

CHORUS. Our god Dionysus, son of Zeus, loves Peace, bestower of prosperity and nursing mother of youth. Equally to rich and poor he grants his bounty, the joy of wine that puts an end to grief . . .

The world's wise, over-ambitious for knowledge, are not really wise, and their time is brief . . .

What is wisdom, or what more precious prize have men from the gods than this—to be victorious over their foes and adore beauty forever? . . .

Happy the man who knows the sacred mysteries, who is pure of life, and whose spirit is inspired by holy revels.

― Reading No. 2 ―

PIONEER SCIENTISTS

Later histories of philosophy, such as Aristotle's survey in the Metaphysics, *include the following fragments from the writings of the physical philosophers or summaries of their ideas.*

✶   ✶   ✶

XENOPHANES

Homer and Hesiod have described the gods as doing all sorts of things that are shameful and disgraceful among men. And men believe that the gods are born like them, wear clothes like them, and have human voice and shape. But if oxen and horses had hands and could produce works of art as men do, they would make their gods in their own image; Ethiopians do make their gods black and snub-nosed, the Thracians make theirs with blue eyes and red hair. Actually there is one god, like men neither in form nor way of thinking, who sees, thinks, and hears in terms of the whole, and himself, eternally unmoving, sets all things in motion by his thought . . . The sea and earth were once one. Evidence of this is the discovery of shells on the mainland in mountain rock.

THALES

Most of the earliest philosophers believed that things originate in some kind of matter. Thales, the first to state this belief, thought that this elemental matter was water. He was also said to be the first to study the heavens and predict eclipses.

ANAXIMINES

The elemental material, one and unlimited, is air, which varies in density and thinness as it changes its form; when rarefied it becomes fire, when condensed it becomes successively cloud, water, earth, and stone. Motion is eternal, and through motion all these changes take place.

HERACLITUS

This world, created by no god or man, was, is, and ever will be an undying fire, kindling and extinguishing itself according to a pattern.

Everything is in motion, nothing stays still; you cannot step twice into the same river.

Conflict is universal, and justice consists of strife; through strife all things come into existence and disappear. A thing which includes strife is at one with itself; harmony arises from opposing tensions, like those of the bow and the lyre. God is day and night, winter and summer, war and peace, surfeit and hunger.

The sun will not overstep his limits; if he does, the Avengers, servants of Justice, will track him down.

Knowledge of many things does not teach understanding. Understanding is to know the thought by which all things are directed.

All human laws are nourished by one divine law.

THE PYTHAGOREANS

In number they thought they could see many similarities to things which are and things which come into being. For example, justice is an arrangement of number, so is life, so is intelligence . . . They concluded that the elements of number are basic to everything; the heavens themselves are a harmony and a ratio.

ANAXIMANDER

Anaximander says that man had his origin in animals of a different species, for all other animals are able to feed themselves early in life, but the human child needs such a long period of nursing that he would not have survived in early times.

HEROIC VIRTUES

The following passages from the Iliad *and* Odyssey
*picture the reckless daring of Achilles when he hears
that his dearest friend, Patroclus, has been killed; the
civic and family responsibility of the Trojan leader,
Hector; and the hospitality offered the shipwrecked
Odysseus by Princess Nausicaa, who has gone with her
maids near the seashore to do the family washing.*

⟋   ⟋   ⟋

a. HOMER: *Iliad* XVIII

When Achilles heard of Patroclus' death a cloud of
grief fell upon him. He poured handfuls of dust over
his head, disfiguring his handsome face and lovely new
tunic; he threw himself on the ground, and in his anguish tore his hair. The captive women screamed in grief
and beat their breasts, bending toward the earth in their
sorrow. Then, as Achilles cried aloud, his mother, Thetis,
heard him as she was sitting in the depths of the sea beside her father, and she, too, started screaming, and the
other sea-nymphs joined her and beat their breasts and
lamented with her.

"Oh my sisters," she cried, "listen to my woe. Sorrow,
sorrow is mine. I bore the most glorious of all sons, I
bore him to be handsome and stalwart, a hero of heroes,
and he grew like a tree, I watched over him as if he
were a precious plant. And then I sent him to Troy to
fight, but I shall never welcome him back to Peleus'
palace. While he lives to look on the sun he is always in
distress, and I cannot help him. But all the same I am
going to see my darling and find out what grieves him
now. He has not been fighting lately, that I know."

She left her cave-home and the other sea-nymphs
came weeping after her, and the waves parted to make
their going easy. When they arrived at the bounteous
Trojan plain they emerged from the sea where the ships

of the Myrmidons were drawn up near Achilles' tents. Then his mother went to him as he lay wailing on the ground, she caressed his head with her hand, and said, "Son, why do you weep so? What trouble has come to you now? Tell me, don't keep it a secret. Surely Zeus did what you prayed him to do, when you asked to have the Achaeans hemmed in at their ships until they realized how much they need you."

Achilles groaned and replied, "Mother, Zeus granted me that request, but what good has it done me, now that my beloved comrade Patroclus is dead? He was more to me than any other friend, I loved him as much as I do life itself. Now he is gone forever, killed by Hector. Oh, how I wish that you had never married Peleus, but he had taken instead a mortal woman as his wife, for now you shall grieve over the death of the son whom you shall never again welcome back home. For I shall not live or come among men unless Hector falls by my spear and pays by his own death for having killed Patroclus."

Thetis wept as she said, "Then, my son, your death, too, is near, for you know it is due to come soon after Hector's."

"I wish I were dead now," said Achilles, "because I could not save my friend. He died far from his home, and when he needed me I was not there to help. What is left for me? I shall go after Hector, and when I have killed him I shall await my doom whenever Zeus and the other gods care to send it. Until it comes, I will win glory, and tears will flow down the cheeks of the Trojan women in grief over their men who have died in battle, and they will know then that he who held back from fighting will hold back no longer. Don't try to restrain me out of your love for me, for you shall not move me."

---

b. HOMER: *Iliad* VI

Hector hurried from his house through the streets toward the Scaean gates, where he was just about to go into the plain when his wife, Andromache, came running to meet him. With her was the nurse, holding in her arms Hector's darling son, lovely as a star. Hector had named him Scamandrios, but all the peole called him Astyanax ("Lord of the City"), because Hector alone was the guardian of Troy. Then Hector smiled and silently gazed at the boy. Andromache stood by weeping, and put her hand on him . . . (*She tries to prevail upon him to stay inside the city and direct its defense, instead of risking death by going out on the plain to fight.*) Noble Hector answered her, "My dear, I, too, have thought of everything you say. But I would be ashamed before the Trojan men and women if like a coward I were to shirk battle. And my own heart doesn't let me do it, for I have learned to be brave and to fight in the front ranks of the Trojans, winning glory for my father and myself. I know well that the day will come when holy Troy shall perish, and with it Priam and his people. But it isn't the agony of the Trojans that grieves me, not even of my mother, Hecuba, or King Priam, or my brothers, many and brave, who will fall in the dust, as much as your bitter sorrow when some bronze-clad Achaean shall lead you away and rob you of your freedom. May the earth be heaped over my body before I hear your cries as they carry you away into slavery."

So spoke noble Hector, and reached his arms out to his son. But the child shrank back with a whimper into the arms of his nurse, afraid of the bronze armor and the horsehair crest nodding terribly on top of the helmet. His father and mother laughed, and Hector took off his helmet and laid it on the ground. Then he kissed his son and dandled him in his arms and spoke in prayer, "Zeus and ye other gods, grant that this son of mine may become, like me, outstanding among the Trojans, as strong as I, and a mighty ruler of men. And may some one say of him as he returns from battle, 'He is a much better man than his father ever was.' May he bring back blood-stained spoils of victory, and make glad the heart of his mother."

Then Hector put the child in the hands of his wife, and she took him to her fragrant bosom, smiling through her tears. Hector pitied her, and caressed her tenderly and said, "Darling, don't be so sad. No man shall send me to Hades before my time comes. But no one has ever escaped his doom, whether he be cowardly or brave, once he has been born. Go home now and keep busy with your tasks there, the loom and the distaff, and overseeing the maids at their work. War is the business of men, for all men here in Troy, but most of all for me."

C. HOMER: *Odyssey* VI

As Odysseus emerged from the bushes, naked and salt-encrusted, the girls were terrified and went racing down the beach. But Nausicaa stayed right where she was, for Athena put courage in her heart and took away her fear. Then Odysseus was at a loss as to whether he should clasp her knees and ask her to help him, or whether he should stay at a distance and merely ask her for some clothes and directions for reaching the city. It seemed better to stay at a distance. So then he began with wheedling words, "I beg you to help me, princess— but first tell me this, are you a goddess or a mortal? If you are one of the goddesses, I imagine you are Artemis. Yes, you are very much like her in looks, size, and figure. But if you are a mortal, most happy are your father and mother, most happy your brothers and sisters! How delighted they must be when they see so radiant a daughter going to a dance! But happiest is the man who will win you with his gifts and lead you to his home as his bride. Now, princess, think of my cruel suffering. Only yesterday I escaped from the wine-dark sea after twenty days of being lashed by waves and winds. Do take pity on me, for I know no one in this country, and point out to me the way to the city and give me a rag to throw about me—perhaps the wrapper in which you did up the washing. In return, I pray the gods to give you whatever your heart longs for—a husband, a home, and a happy marriage. For there is nothing more pleasant than when a man and his wife live together and understand each other. It irritates their enemies, delights their friends, and they themselves know better than anyone else how good it is."

Nausicaa answered, "Stranger, you seem to me a very sensible person. Of course Olympian Zeus allots good and

bad fortune to men as he wishes, and he has given you
these troubles, which you must endure. But now that
you have come to our country you will not lack clothing
or anything else that a man in trouble deserves to get
when he asks for help. I will show you the way to the
city and tell you who live there. We are Phaeacians, and
the king is Alcinous, and I am his daughter."

Then she called to her maids, "Stop! Why are you
running off like that when you see a man? He's no enemy
of ours, for there is no one who will make war on us,
dear as we are to the immortal gods and living so far
away from the rest of the world. This man is just a poor
wanderer who has strayed here and deserves our help,
for strangers and beggars are under Zeus' protection.
So give him something to eat and drink, and bathe him
in the river in a place sheltered from the wind." At that
the maids stopped running and called to one another to
come back. Then they led Odysseus to a sheltered place,
as Nausicaa had directed, brought him clothes to wear,
gave him a golden flask of oil, and told him to take his
bath in the river.

Odysseus washed the brine from his back and broad
shoulders and hair, and rubbed his body with oil and
put on the clothes. And then Athena made him look
taller and more stalwart than before, she even made the
hair grow thick on the top of his head and flow down
like hyacinth blossoms, and she shed beauty and grace
about him. Oh, he was handsome and radiant to see as
he came and sat down on the sand. And when she saw
him Nausicaa couldn't stop looking at him, and she said
to the maids, "Listen, my dears. I believe the gods who
live on Olympus have sent this man here. When I first
saw him I thought he looked rather plain, but now he
resembles the gods who live in heaven. If only he would
stay here, for it's a person like him whom I'd like for
a husband. Oh well, give him something to eat and
drink." So they did as she commanded and served
Odysseus with food and wine.

COMMON SENSE AND INGENUITY

As early as the heroic age the common man had a right to speak his mind, as when Thersites in public assembly criticized Agamemnon, his commander-in-chief. In the eighth century Hesiod spoke for the oppressed farmers. By the sixth century Aesop had written and collected fables which illustrate everyday common sense, and in the Homeric Hymn to Hermes, *an anonymous poet praised by implication the skill and tact of the rising mercantile class, of which Hermes was the patron god. Even if their ethics were sometimes questionable, their ingenuity was praiseworthy.*

✔   ✔   ✔

a. HOMER: *Iliad* II

Now all the rest were seated in an orderly fashion in their places, but Thersites kept ranting on, an endless talker, with a mind full of subversive ideas and opposition to those in authority. He was the ugliest of all the men who came to Troy: bow-legged, lame in one foot, his shoulders hunched over his chest, and his head rising to a point with only a little fuzz growing on the top of it. He was most obnoxious to Achilles and Odysseus, for he used to revile them constantly, but now it was noble Agamemnon whom he shrilly accused. The Achaeans were indignant and disgusted with him, but he kept bawling his criticism of Agamemnon at the top of his lungs. "Son of Atreus, what's the matter now, and what more do you want? Your tents are full of bronze and the pick of the women we give you whenever we Achaeans seize a town. Or don't you have gold enough, brought by some horse-taming Trojan as ransom for his son, after it was I or some other soldier who took him prisoner? Or is it a young girl you're looking for, to keep to yourself and enjoy? (*turning to the soldiers*) I say it's not right for our commander to bring misery on us. Oh you weaklings,

cowards, women, not men! I say let's go home and leave
him here at Troy to profit from his precious prizes and
find out whether we're of any use to him or not. Now
he has insulted Achilles, a much better man than he is.
He has grabbed Achilles' girl away from him. If Achilles
resented it the way he should (*turning to the king*), son
of Atreus, you'd never live to insult him again!"

---

b. HESIOD: *Works and Days*

After Prometheus had deceived Zeus by bringing fire
from heaven to men, Zeus said to him, "So you rejoice in
having stolen fire and deceived me! It shall be disastrous
to you and to men in the future. For I shall give them
evil to offset the fire, and they shall delight in it and hug
it to their hearts." Then he laughed merrily, and ordered
Hephaestus to mix earth with water and put in it human
voice and strength and make its face like the immortal
goddesses, the face of a lovely maiden; he ordered Athena
to teach her the useful arts of weaving, and golden
Aphrodite to shed about her head grace that inspires
painful longing and desires that weaken limbs; and he
ordered Hermes to give her a shameless mind and tricky
ways. So he commanded, and they obeyed Zeus; and this
woman he called Pandora, because all the gods living on
Olympus gave her a gift. And she was to be the bane
of men.

I wish I had not been born in this fifth race of men,
but either had died before it or been born after it. For
now we are a race of iron, which never ceases from
labor and sorrow. And as time goes on there will be no
kindness between kin, between guest and host, between
friend and friend. No honor will be paid parents as they
grow old and frail; instead, their children will criticize
them and treat them cruelly. There will be no respect
for the man who keeps his promises, nor for men who
are just and good, but arrogant and evil men will receive
honor. Might will be regarded as right. Better men will
be injured by crafty and lying ones; malice and envy
will be rife among wretched mortals. Then the divine

spirits of self-respect and consideration for others and just retribution will veil their faces and abandon this earth for heaven, leaving only misery for men and no refuge from disaster.

———

Before success the gods have set sweat. . . . Do not put off work until tomorrow. . . . Hunger is a fit comrade for an idler. . . . Befriend the man who befriends you, and oppose the one who opposes you. . . . It is good to take in moderation from a neighbor, but it is also good to repay him the same amount, and more if you can, so that if later you are in need you may rely on him for help. . . . The man who harms another harms himself, and evil planned harms most him who planned it. . . . Little time has a man for law suits unless he has a year's victuals stored up. . . . Don't be taken in by a woman, it's your barn that she's after. . . . Even with your brother, smile but bring along a witness. . . . Keep to the middle way, moderation is best. . . . Zeus has decreed this law: although fish and animals and birds should eat one another, for justice is not in them, mankind has been given justice, a far better way of life.

———

c. AESOP: *Fables*

A camel, forced by his master to dance, said, "Of course I'm no good at dancing. Even when I walk I'm awkward."

———

A mosquito settled on a bull's horn and stayed there for some time. When he was about to fly away he asked the bull, "Are you willing for me to leave now?" The bull replied, "When you came I didn't notice it, and I won't notice it if you go."

———

A groom stole the horse's grain and sold it, but kept rubbing down and currying the horse every day. The horse said, "If you want me really to look well, don't sell my barley."

———

A dog chased a hare and overcame it. Now it would take a nip at the hare, then wag its tail and caress it. The hare said, "If you are friendly, why do you bite me? If you are hostile, why do you wag your tail?"

―――――

While wandering along the seashore a lion saw a dolphin swimming, and invited him to make an alliance, saying that it was right for them to be friends and help one another. "For you," he said, "are the king of sea creatures and I of those on land." The dolphin gladly agreed. A little later the lion got into a fight with a savage bull and kept calling upon the dolphin for help. When the dolphin, though eager, was not able to come out from the sea, the lion reproached him for being a traitor. But the dolphin said, "Don't blame me. Blame Nature, which made me a sea creature and doesn't allow me to come on land."

―――――

d. ANON.: *Homeric Hymn to Hermes*

A hymn to Hermes, the son of Zeus and Maia, that clever child, that cunning schemer, that thief of cattle. Born at dawn, by noon he had invented the lyre and in the evening he stole the cattle of Apollo. . . . (*He jumped from his cradle, killed a tortoise at the doorway of his cave-home and made a lyre out of it, then, hungry for roast beef, he set out for the meadows where Apollo kept his prize cows. He picked out fifty of them and drove them away backwards to a mountain glen, swishing along himself on bundles of brushwood, so as to confuse any pursuer. Then he slaughtered the cattle, roasted the meat, stored it away for future use, destroyed all obvious evidence, and returned to his cradle. On the following day Apollo visited his herd and discovered the theft; suspecting Hermes he went to the cave, which he searched thoroughly without avail before confronting the baby.*)

"You baby in the cradle," Apollo said, "tell me where my cattle are, right away, or I shall hurl you to black Tartarus, and neither your father nor your mother will be able to bring you back to the light."

Hermes answered him with shrewd words: "Apollo, what in the world do you mean by such rough talk? Why have you come here looking for your cattle? I've seen nothing and heard nothing about them. I couldn't even accept an informer's reward. And do I look like a cattle thief, a husky fellow? No, that's no concern of mine. My business is sleep, my mother's milk, warm blankets and hot baths. I strongly advise you not to let any one know that you have made such an accusation; the gods would be astounded at the very idea of a new-born baby stealing and bringing home a herd of cattle. It's ridiculous! I was born only yesterday, my feet are too tender for any such rough going. If you want I'll swear a great oath, by my father's head: I solemnly swear I am not guilty and do not know who may have stolen your cattle—whatever cattle may be, for I have only heard tell of them." While he said this his eyes kept darting here and there and his head shook from side to side and he made little whistling noises.

Apollo replied, "Son, you are a trickster and you have a heart full of deceit. I expect you'll do plenty of stealing as you grow older, judging from the way you've talked now, and you will be called the Prince of Thieves." (*Apollo then took him up to Olympus and charged him with the crime before Zeus as judge. Hermes denied the charge.*)

"Father Zeus, I will tell you the truth, for I cannot tell a lie. Apollo came to our house this morning looking for some of his cattle. He brought no witnesses, but demanded, using force and threats of hurling me to Tartarus, that I confess to stealing them. Of course he is a stalwart young man, and I am a baby born only yesterday, as he very well knows. I certainly don't look like a cattle thief, a husky fellow! Believe me, father—for you say you are my father—I did not drive his cattle to my house, I did not even step over the threshold of the cave. So as to be rich some day it's the truth I'm telling you. I revere the sun and I love you, but I hate *him*. You know I am innocent, and besides I'll now swear a solemn oath: I am not guilty, and some day I shall make this person pay for the outrageous way he has treated me, even if he is the stronger. Do you, father, help the weak and helpless." (*Zeus, of course, knew what had actually happened, and laughed, admiring his little son's skill and ingenuity. He told the two of them to settle their differences in the spirit of conciliation; whereupon Hermes showed consumate tact as well as shrewdness in giving Apollo the lyre he had invented and thereby getting the good will of the god.*)

"Apollo I do not begrudge you the use of this lyre, in fact you will become proficient in playing it this very day. Of course you are all-wise, you sit on a front seat among the gods, you are sturdy and powerful. Zeus loves you, and no wonder, and he has given you precious gifts—the power of knowing the oracles and prophecies that come from Zeus himself. But as far as this art of music is concerned, I welcome your learning it to your heart's content. Since you feel like playing the lyre, play it, sing to it, enjoy it. Just please remember that I gave it to you, and let me have some of the glory. Here is the lyre, take it, it is yours."

— Reading No. 5 —

POETIC INSIGHT

In the seventh and sixth centuries poets, chiefly in the Ionian cities of Asia Minor and the islands of the Aegean sea, invented forms of lyric poetry to express their intimate personal feelings on such subjects as patriotism, nature, love, and wine. Among the chief poets were Tyrtaeus, Archilochus, Alcman, Alcaeus, Anacreon, Theognis, and Sappho.

✦   ✦   ✦

TYRTAEUS

Noble is the man who falls in battle, bravely fighting for his native land. But wretched is the man without a country.

———

ARCHILOCHUS

Some Thracian struts with my shield—I threw it in a bush as I fled. It was a good shield, but I'm still alive to fight again with another shield just as good.

———

ALCMAN

Asleep are the mountaintops and valleys, ridges and ravines; the creeping things in the dark earth, the beasts that live on the hills, the race of bees, the great fish in the depths of the purple sea, all are asleep, and asleep are the tribes of long-winged birds.

———

ALCAEUS

Not well-roofed houses or sturdy walls or canals or dockyards make a city. A city is made by men who have the ability to seize their opportunities.

———

The sailors (of our ship of state) have thrown their entire cargo overboard and are trying to save their lives, while the ship, lashed by the waves, has nearly given up the fight and would willingly hit a reef and sink. But as for me, dear comrades, I would like to forget all that and make merry here with you and Bacchus. And yet we must cherish our country, even though fools have brought her to confusion.

———

ANACREON

I dined on a bit of wheat cake, I drank a whole jug of wine, and now I strum softly on my lute a serenade to my sweetheart.

THEOGNIS

Have nothing to do with inferior men, but associate only with the well-born. Eat and drink with them, stay beside them and study how to please them. That is the part of wisdom; but those who associate with base men lose their wisdom.

Many base men are rich and men of noble birth are poor; but we will not exchange our virtue for their wealth, for money goes now here, now there, but virtue always abides steadfast.

SAPPHO

That man seems to me like a god who sits beside you and listens to your sweet chatter, and your lovely laughter, which sets my heart beating wildly. For when I look at you my voice leaves me, my tongue is frozen, and a piercing flame pervades my flesh, my eyes are blurred and my ears ring, sweat pours down me, I tremble all over, I become paler than grass, and I feel I am nearly dying.

Atthis, our beloved Anactoria now lives far away in Sardis, but often she sends over the severing sea her loving thoughts. And she remembers how we used to be together, and how she loved your singing, and you were like a goddess to her. Now, among the girls in Lydia, she is as radiant as the rosy-fingered moon, which outshines all the stars and sheds its light over the salt sea and the flowering fields, when the dew lies on the grass, and the roses and the delicate anthryse and honey-sweet clover are in bloom. And even if she is far from us, I know she remembers Atthis' love for her, and her heart is aching with loneliness, and she cries for us to come— and Night hears her cries and brings them to us across the severing sea.

———

Evening, you bring home all that the shining dawn scattered: you bring home the sheep, you bring home the goat, you bring home the child to its mother.

———

She is like the sweet apple that reddens upon the top bough, high on the very highest one, which the pickers forgot. Oh no, they didn't forget it, they couldn't reach it!

———

Mother, I cannot tend my weaving, for I am overcome by Aphrodite with longing for my slender lover.

———

Around the lovely moon the radiant beauty of the stars grows dim when she at the full sheds her silver light over the earth.

———

The moon and the Pleiads have set, it is midnight, and I lie alone.

———

Love has unbound my limbs and made me tremble, sweet-bitter Love.

———

Harbinger of Spring, longing-voiced nightingale.

EVOLVING RELIGION

The chorus of old men in the Agamemnon *by Aeschylus (525-456) trying to justify the ways of gods to men, declare that men learn through suffering and transgressors are punished. Pindar (518-438) went beyond earlier notions of the after-life in picturing, in one of his odes in honor of athletes, how men of honor live after death in the Isle of the Blest.*

✓   ✓   ✓

a. AESCHYLUS: *Agamemnon*

CHORUS. Zeus, whoever he is, if by this name he wishes to be called, by this name I will call him. There is no one comparable to Zeus for comfort, when I reflect upon the whole of experience and try to rid myself of the bitter sorrow which eats at my heart. No god who formerly was great will even be spoken of now. But Zeus is the name to invoke if one is to win the boon of wisdom—Zeus who, setting us on our road, made this the law of life, "Men must learn through suffering." So, drop by drop, in sleep upon the heart falls the heavy memory of pain. Against one's will comes wisdom. This grace of the gods is forced upon us by powers who themselves became supreme only after bitter struggle.

———

CHORUS. Omnipotent Zeus, you encircled with a net those towers of Troy so that none could escape, all were trapped in the wide coils of doom.

Zeus, God of Hospitality, him I praise because he punished the transgressor, shooting with unerring accuracy so that the arrow would not miss its mark.

It has been truly said that Zeus tracks down and smites the sinner, such is his will. When men say that God pays no heed to those who trample underfoot his holy laws, they lie. For swift ruin comes on men who, puffed up with arrogant pride and wealth beyond measure, insult the altar of Justice. When such a one prays, none in heaven hears his cry, but Justice drags him down to death. So with Paris, who came to the home of Menelaus and betrayed his host's hospitality by taking Helen away.

————

b. PINDAR: *Olympian* 2

The souls of good men win a life of happiness with lightened toil, enjoying sunshine by both day and night; and those who gladly kept their promises live on without tears (but those who broke them suffer hideous torments). Men who bravely stood firm and refrained from injustice walk a divine road to a place where breezes from the ocean gently blow about the Isle of the Blest. There gleam golden flowers, some on shining trees, others on the water; and the blest wear wreaths of the flowers on their heads as they enjoy the righteous laws of the greatest of judges.

— Reading No. 7 —

EVOLVING SCIENCE

Speculation on the physical nature of the universe continued during the fifth century, resulting in theories which included those of elements, the atom, and kinetic energy. Only fragments of the writings of these theoretical scientists remain. Principles of scientific medicine were formulated and practiced by Hippocrates (c. 425), whose case histories and physician's oath are preserved along with the medical observations of many of his followers.

✓   ✓   ✓

PARMENIDES

"Being is real, non-Being is impossible." This is a reasonable statement, but to say that there are of necessity things that do not exist is absurd; for how can one know about a nonexistent thing? Being is without beginning or end; it includes everything, is immovable and eternal, one continuous whole. How could it have been created? From what could it have come into existence, and how? It cannot have come from nothing.

EMPEDOCLES

There are four elements: fire, air, earth, and water. There is no beginning or end of things, there is only mixture and separation of these elements. Sometimes a unity develops out of many things, and sometimes a whole separates into many parts. Such change goes on continuously. Love is the force that brings things together, Strife the force that separates them. Thus One keeps developing from Many and Many from the division of One.

ANAXAGORAS

All things include portions of every kind of matter, but Mind alone is infinite, self-controlled, subject only to itself. It governs all other matter, being itself the finest and purest of matter. Mind started the universe rotating; Mind determined the mixing and separation of matter; Mind decided the number of everything past, present, and future; it established the course of the heavenly bodies; it caused the rotation that separated thick from thin, warm from cold, light from darkness, dry from moist.

LEUCIPPUS

Atoms (indivisible particles) and their countless combinations are the elements of everything; they are unlimited in number, and are in continuous motion. The solid and compact atoms may be defined as "Being," and they move through empty Space, which may be called "Not-Being."

HIPPOCRATES

The so-called "sacred disease" (epilepsy) has natural causes like other disease. No disease is beyond being understood or incapable of being cured.

The material on which medicine works has always been right at hand, and methods have been worked out by which many important discoveries have been made. What is still undiscovered will be found out if those who study it are competent.

To understand disease we must study the general nature of mankind, individual differences, the disease itself, the treatments used, and the doctor who applies them. The more we know of such matters, the easier it will be to make a sound judgment. Climate and local peculiarities of weather must be considered; then the particular patient—his habits, occupation, and age; his manner of talking and keeping silent; his temperament; his sleep or inability to sleep; the time and type of his dreams; his gestures, his tears. Finally we must record during the course of the disease the movements of the bowels and the urine, the spitting and vomiting; we must follow every stage of the disease and note what occurs and the result in recovery or death. During its course we must observe carefully every detail so as to decide what direction the disease will take.

A Case History. Name: Philiscus. Residence: near the city wall. The first day he had an acute fever with sweating, went to bed, was distressed all night. Second day: worse, but took an enema and got some sleep. Third day: he seemed to be over his fever in the morning, but in the afternoon it came on again, higher than before; sweating, thirst, parched tongue, dark-colored urine. Had a bad night, sleepless and delirious. Fourth day: worse, urine still dark, but he felt more comfortable at night. Fifth day: slight nosebleed, granules in urine, small bowel movement after taking laxative. Bad night, delirium, extremities cold. Toward morning he got some sleep. Hereafter unable to speak. Heavy sweat, extremities turning grayish color. Sixth day: died at noon, after period of slow, painful breathing. His spleen was swollen. Disease marked by cold sweats. He felt worse every even-numbered day.

The Hippocratic Oath.—I swear by Apollo and the other divinities of healing that according to my ability I will keep this oath: to regard the man who taught me the art of medicine as dear to me as my own parents; to follow that system of treatment which I believe will help my patients, and to refrain from anything that is harmful to them. I will give no deadly drug if I am asked to do so, nor will I recommend any such thing; I will not practice abortion. In purity and holiness I will practice the art of medicine. Whatever I see or hear which should not be divulged, I will keep secret. While I continue to keep this oath may I enjoy life and the practice of my profession, respected at all times by all men.

— Reading No. 8 —

SOPHISTS AND IDEALISTS

In reaction against materialistic conclusions there were two groups of philosophers during the fifth and fourth centuries: the Sophists, and the idealists Socrates, Plato and Aristotle. Sophists believed that the perfecting of human communication for practical success should be the chief subject of study. The idealists believed that men

*should try to understand the moral intelligence which
governs the universe.*

✦   ✦   ✦

a. SOPHISTS

Protagoras said that man is the measure of all things,
of the existence of those things that exist and of the
nonexistence of those that do not. (Aristotle: *Metaphysics*)

Regarding the gods, I (Protagoras) do not know
whether they exist or not, or of what their nature may
be. For many things keep me from knowing—the ob-
scurity of the subject, and the brevity of life.

———

SOCRATES. If this friend of mine becomes your pupil,
Protagoras, in what respect will he become a better man?

PROTAGORAS. Socrates, your question is a reasonable
one, and I am happy to answer it. If he comes to learn
of me, he will not be treated as other Sophists treat
their pupils, with a routine course of study in mathematics, astronomy, literature, music, and speech. No,
from me he will learn how to manage efficiently his
private affairs and acquire such an understanding of public affairs as to fit him for a successful career as a citizen and statesman.

———

Hippias was surrounded by students he had brought
with him from various cities, and they were questioning
him about the philosophy of nature and astronomy.
(Plato: *Protagoras*)

———

b. PLATO: *Phaedo*

SOCRATES. When I was a young man I was eager to
understand the natural world—how animals are formed,
what produces perception, the nature of the heavens and
earth, and many other similar phenomena. Then I heard
a person reading from a book by Anaxagoras which said

that it is intelligence which sets everything in order and is the cause of all things, and I was delighted; it seemed to me a fine thing that intelligence ordered everything for the best. So I was happy to have found in Anaxagoras a teacher of the causes of things, showing how they came to be as they are and that it is best for them to be as they are. From this wonderful hope I was speedily thrown down, for as I read his books I found that he defined intelligence in purely materialistic and nonmoral terms. It was as if one should say that I, Socrates, am sitting here because my body is composed of bones and sinews and joints, and from their interaction I now sit as I do, omitting to tell the real cause, that since it seemed best to the Athenians to condemn me, I thought it best to sit here and submit to the punishment. For by the dog (*i.e.*, the dog-star, Sirius) I think these sinews and bones of mine would have been off long since to some other country, if I had not thought it more just and honorable to submit to my sentence than to run away. Of course I could not do as I wish without bones and sinews; but to say that I do as I do because of them, and not from a choice of what I think is best, is an unreasonable way of speaking.

C. PLATO

Did the universe always exist, or was it created? Since it is visible and tangible and has material substance we conclude that it was created. What is created must necessarily be created by a cause. . . .

God did not make material first and the soul afterwards; in origin and value he made the soul prior to material in order to rule it. . . .

As the final stage in the pattern of the universe the Creator contrived four species: heavenly gods, the birds of the air, the fish of the waters, and land animals. The heavenly creatures he created chiefly out of fire, so that they might be brightest and most beautiful. And he instructed them to imitate him and create the other species, by mixing portions of fire, earth, water, and air. These are the elements with which the self-sufficient and perfect Creator associated himself as his ministers in creating his work, which was for the good of his creation. So the universe has received creatures, mortal and immortal, and has become a creation expressing the Creator, who is the image of the intellectual, the greatest, the most beautiful, and the best. (*Timaeus*)

———

This parable (of the cave) I ask you to apply to our previous discussion (of the relation of the world of sensation to the world of ideas, which we comprehend by reasoning processes). We may compare the cave to the world which we perceive by sight, and the journey upward from it and the contemplation of the world of sunlight we may compare to the journey of the soul into the world of Ideas. Whether this is true or not, God knows, but that is how it seems to me. In the world of Ideas the final thing to be comprehended, and that not easily, is the Idea of the Good; but once it is comprehended, one must conclude that it is the cause of everything just and lovely. . . . Every man's soul has this power of comprehension, but it must turn from the world of becoming and look upon that brightest of Being, the Good. (*Republic* VII)

———

d. ARISTOTLE

We believe that we possess scientific knowledge of a thing when we think we know its cause. (*Posterior Analytics*)

We must acquire knowledge of original causes, of which there are four: the material cause (*e.g.*, the bronze of the statue); the formal cause (*e.g.*, the ratio 2:1 and number generally are causes of the octave); the efficient cause (*e.g.*, the father is the cause of the child); and the final cause (*e.g.*, the purpose served, as health is a cause of walking). (*Metaphysics*)

Evidently there is a first cause. Since continuous motion exists, there must be something eternal that first imparts motion, and this must itself be unmoved. And insofar as it is necessary it is good. Such a principle governs the heavens and the natural world. (*Physics*)

Our ancestors from long ago handed down to us the tradition that the essential substances of the universe are gods, and that all nature is divine. Religious tradition later added to this certain myths, in order to persuade the people and provide for practical social expediency, to the effect that these gods are in the form of men or other earthly creatures. If, however, we were to take only the original assumption—that the essential substances are divine—we would have to consider that an inspired statement. (*Metaphysics*)

God is always in that state of contemplation which is most pleasurable and best. Life belongs to God; for the existence of thought is life, and God is that existence, and God's essential being is life most good and eternal. So we say that God is a being eternal and perfect, and that life and continuous duration belong to God. (*Physics*)

Every part of nature is wonderful, and we should study every kind of animal life without aversion; for all will show us something natural and beautiful. The lack of chance and the direction of every part to a definite end are present in all the works of nature. (*De Partibus Animalium*)

All natural products serve an end. This is most clearly seen in creatures other than man. The swallow, for example, makes its nest and the spider spins its web for a purpose; plants grow leaves to protect the fruit from the sun, and send their roots down for nourishment. This final cause applies to everything in nature. (*Physics*)

THUCYDIDES: PERICLES' FUNERAL SPEECH

In 430, after the first year of the war between Athens and the coalition of Sparta, Corinth, and Thebes, a state funeral was held for the Athenian soldiers who had died during that year. Pericles was chosen to give the funeral oration. Here it is as reported by Thucydides in his History of the Peloponnesian War, II.

Most of the previous speakers at this ceremony have praised the custom of having an address. They have considered it fitting that the men who died in battle should be so commemorated. I do not share that feeling. In my opinion deeds deserve deeds, not words, to honor them. But since custom has determined that an address should be made, I must abide by the custom and speak to the best of my ability in a way satisfactory to you.

I shall speak first of our ancestors. It is right and fitting that on such an occasion we should remember them; for, living here, generation after generation, they handed down to us because of their efforts a country that is free. So they deserve our praise. And our own fathers deserve it even more, for they labored to add to Athens the empire which we now possess. And we ourselves, those of us who are in middle age, have contributed to make the city self-sufficient both in war and peace.

The various wars and military campaigns by which we rose to greatness I shall not recount; you know the story well. Instead, I will describe the way of life which led to our success, the form of government and the kind of character that have made Athens great.

Our government is called a democracy because power resides, not in a few people, but in the majority of our citizens. But every person has equal rights before the law; prestige and respect are paid those who win them by their merits, regardless of their political, economic, or social status; and no one is deprived of making his contribution to the city's welfare. We are equally fair-minded in tolerating differences in people's private concerns; we do not get irritated with our neighbors when they do what they like or show those signs of disapproval which do no great harm but are certainly unpleasant. In our public dealings we have respect for our officials and the laws, especially those laws which protect the helpless and those unwritten laws whose violation is generally regarded as shameful.

But we do more than this. We have provided for the happiness of our people many recreations: athletic games, contests of various sorts, festivals throughout the year, and beautiful buildings to cheer the heart and refresh the spirit as we see them every day. Also we enjoy imported goods from all over the world, which add to the attractive variety of our life.

As far as preparing for war is concerned we are much better off than our enemies. Our city is open to the world, and we have no regular deportations to keep foreigners from learning what might be of use to an enemy. For we have confidence in our native resourcefulness rather than in mere military strength. Our enemies have a rigid system for cultivating courage from their youth onward, but we, doing pretty much as we please, are as well prepared as they when danger arises. If we choose such a varied way of life instead of constant military drill, and rely on native ingenuity rather than state-made courage, we have a double advantage over them. We do not become worn out beforehand, and when danger does arise we are as courageous as our plodding rivals.

We love beauty without extravagance, and wisdom without weakness of will. Wealth we regard not as a means for private display but rather for public service; and poverty we consider no disgrace, although we think it is a disgrace not to try to overcome it. We believe a man should be concerned about public as well as private affairs, for we regard the person who takes no part in politics not as merely uninterested but as useless. We reach decisions on public policy only after full discussion, believing that sound judgment, far from being impeded by discussion, is arrived at only when full information is considered before a decision is made.

To sum it up, I claim that our city is a model for all Greece and that here more than anywhere else a man can become independent in spirit, versatile in accomplishment, and richly developed in personality. The proof of our greatness is the way in which we have made our way into every land and sea, establishing memorials of our hostility and our favor.

Such is the city for which these men died, exulting in their determination that she should not perish. It is fitting that we who survive should likewise spend ourselves in her service. We may pray to be spared their suffering, but we cannot be less brave than they. We must not be content with words—how fine a thing it is to defend Athens against her enemies—but must fall in love with our city as we see her engaging in her everyday activities, and remember that it was men like these who made her great because of their courage, their understanding of their duty, and their self-discipline in performing it.

By giving their lives they have won for themselves glory that shall never fade, and the greatest of all memorials, not that in which their bodies are laid to rest, but memory in the minds of men, to stimulate future generations in other lands to thought and action. Your duty now is to rival what they have done, remembering that happiness depends on freedom, and freedom is won and preserved by courage.

To those who mourn here today for their loved ones, I say, be of good courage. For you know that life is a matter of fortune, good and bad, and the most fortunate are those who get a noble death, like these men, or a noble grief, like yours. It will be hard for you to believe this, I know; in seeing others happy in their families you will be reminded of the happiness that you once enjoyed, but you parents must hope to have other children, those of you who are not too old to do so; other children will help you forget those who have died, and they will provide greater security for our city. As for you who are beyond your prime, reckon the part of your lives already past as gain, and remember that only a short time is left, and its burdens will be lightened by the glorious memory of the dead.

Finally, if I must say a word to those of you who are now bereft of your husbands, about the virtues of women, I will sum it up in this way: your reputation is best when you maintain the standards of true womanhood and when you give men the least occasion either to praise or blame you.

I have complied with the custom and said what I thought should be said. As for deeds, the funeral honors have now been paid our fallen soldiers, and, as you know, the city will provide for their children until they come of age. That is the reward the city pays for such service; and properly, for the best men serve the city which serves them best.

And now, when you have finished your lamentations, let each of you depart.

— Reading No. 10 —

THUCYDIDES ON REVOLUTION

In Book III of his History *Thucydides analyzed the motives and actions involved in party strife within city-states.*

✓   ✓   ✓

Revolution wrought terrible calamities in the cities of Greece, such have existed and always will exist as long as human nature remains as it is, but which change in character under varying conditions. In times of peace and prosperity states and individuals, not subject to imperious necessity, are governed in accordance with higher motives; but war, taking away the comforts of life, is a hard master and molds men's characters to fit their circumstances.

As the revolutionary spirit grew in intensity, men surpassed their predecessors in the ingenuity of their plots and the brutality of their revenge. Words no longer meant what they had before, but were distorted to serve personal and party purposes: recklessness was called loyal courage; prudent delay, cowardice; restraint, weakness of will; frantic energy, true manliness. The ties of party were stronger than those of family, because a partisan would act without daring to ask why. No agreements were binding if there was an opportunity of breaking them successfully. For party associations, it should be understood, are not based on law nor do they seek the common welfare; they are lawless and seek only self-interest.

The cause of all these evils was greed, ambition, and lust for power, and the party spirit which they created. Leaders of one faction would pretend to uphold democratic equality, the other the superior wisdom of an aristocracy, whereas in reality both considered only what profit they could make for themselves at the expense of the people. They committed the most atrocious crimes with complete disregard of any process of law. Religion meant nothing to either group, but it was cynically used for selfish purposes. Those who belonged to neither party became the prey of both.

— Reading No. 11 —

MINORITY RIGHTS

Pericles included in his Funeral Speech a reference to individual and minority rights. In the Acharnians *the comedian Aristophanes spoke for the anti-democratic and anti-war minority. Sophocles, in the* Antigone, *pointed up the conflict between authority and the individual con-*

science; Antigone believes it is her sacred as well as her family duty to bury her brother's body, because his soul will never find rest in the lower world until the proper ceremony of burial has been performed. One leading minority consisted of women. Euripides' Medea is a tragic portrayal of a woman who punishes a faithless husband. Aristophanes, in the Ecclesiazusae, *represented women masquerading as men in order to vote to hand over the government to women. Plato, in the* Republic, *unequivocally declared for women's rights.*

✔   ✔   ✔

a. ARISTOPHANES: *Knights* and *Acharnians*

(*In the* Knights *a general is trying to persuade a sausage-seller, to unseat Cleon, the democratic leader.*)

SAUSAGE SELLER. Tell me this, how can I, a sausage-seller, be a big man like that?

GENERAL. The easiest thing in the world. You've got all the qualifications: low birth, marketplace training, insolence.

SAUSAGE SELLER. I don't think I deserve it.

GENERAL. Not deserve it? It looks to me as if you've got too good a conscience. Was your father a gentleman?

SAUSAGE SELLER. By the gods, no! My folks were scoundrels.

GENERAL. Lucky man! What a good start you've got for public life!

SAUSAGE SELLER. But I can hardly read.

GENERAL. The only trouble is that you know anything. To be a leader of the people isn't for learned men, or honest men, but for the ignorant and vile. Don't miss this golden opportunity.

———

(*In the* Archarnians, *Dicaeopolis* (Honest Citizen) *is pictured as a sensible farmer who makes a private peace of his own with Sparta. This is resented by a group of poor charcoal burners from rural Acharnia, who want to stone him to death as a traitor but finally consent to listen to his explanation.*)

DICAEOPOLIS. My good men, listen to the terms of my treaty and see if they aren't reasonable.

ACHARNIANS. How can they be? Sparta doesn't keep any promises.

DICAEOPOLIS. I know the Spartans, too, and even if we hate them we'll have to admit they aren't entirely to blame for the mess Athens is in.

ACHARNIANS. Not entirely? Not entirely? You dare to say things like that and expect to be spared?

DICAEOPOLIS. Not entirely to blame, I say, and if you'd give me a chance I could prove that we have wronged them. I hate them, to be sure, for they have cut down my vines as well as yours. Yet, since we are all friends here, let's ask ourselves why we blame the Spartans for our troubles. It's our own leaders—not the people of Athens, they're not to blame—but rascals among us, counterfeit statesmen, worthless, spurious men, who kept denouncing imports from Megara and put an embargo on them. That was a trifling matter, the way we regularly conduct our foreign affairs. But then some of our young bloods stole a prostitute from Megara, and the Megarians retaliated by abducting two of the light women in the house run by Aspasia. Then our Olympian Pericles thundered and lightninged so as to stir up all Hellas, the Megarians begged the Spartans to help them, and the Spartans asked us to remove the embargo, but of course we wouldn't yield an inch. Then the war was on. Some of you will say the Spartans shouldn't have done what they did. But you know that if somebody stole a puppy from one of your island allies you would go to war about it.

---

b. SOPHOCLES: *Antigone*

CREON. Tell me at once and to the point: Did you know that my edict forbade burial of your brother's body?

ANTIGONE. Of course. How could I help knowing? It was made perfectly clear.

CREON. And you dared to disobey it?

ANTIGONE. Yes, for it was not Zeus who issued that edict, and Justice who lives with the gods below never made any such law. And I could not believe that an edict of yours, since you are only a man, could over-rule the unwritten, eternal laws of the gods. Those laws live forever—yesterday, today, tomorrow. So, revering them, I would not for fear of any man invite divine judgment. I know that I must die. Why not? Even though you never made such an edict I would have to die; and if now I die before my time I shall gain by it. For when one lives as I have in the midst of suffering, how can death be anything but gain? No, dying will not hurt me. But if I had left my brother's body unburied that would have hurt me. And if I seem to you to be a fool in what I am doing, perhaps you who judge me are the fool.

---

c. EURIPIDES: *Medea*

MEDEA. Women of Corinth, I ask you to be kind to me, because a blow has fallen on me which has ruined my life. There is no more happiness for me, I want only to die. My husband, on whom I relied for all my happiness, has betrayed me.

Of all living things we women surely are the most wretched. First we must get together a large dowry to buy a husband, and then it's a master of our bodies that we get. Not to have one brings even more unhappiness. Then comes the greatest gamble of all—will he be kind or cruel? You know how hard it is for women to secure a divorce, and it is impossible to reject a husband. So, entering on a new way of life, a bride must be a seer —she never learned those things at home—to get on well with this man who sleeps beside her. If we work our hardest we may manage it so that our husbands stay with us without fretting—then life is enviable. But if we fail, we were better dead. When a man finds life unbearable at home he goes out to visit some friend, or to his club, and finds relief. But we have only him to turn to. Then they say that we lead a sheltered life, that we avoid danger, while they go out to fight. Non-sense! I'd rather go three times into battle than bear one child.

---

d. ARISTOPHANES: *Ecclesiazusae*

ASSEMBLY "MAN." How women are better in running things than we are I'll now explain. First, they dip their wool in boiling dyes, in the good old-fashioned way. You won't see them trying new-fangled methods. And wouldn't Athens have been safe if she had let well enough alone and not always tried something new? Women sit down when they roast grain just as they used to do. They carry burdens on their heads just as they used to do. They observe their festivals just as they used to do. They pester their husbands just as they used to do. They buy themselves dainties just as they used to do. They take their wine strong just as they used to do. They enjoy making love just as they used to do. So, men, let us hand over the city to them and not even guess; let alone try to find out, what they intend to do, but wholeheartedly let them govern, having decided that they, being mothers, will be eager to keep their soldier sons safe. And who could supply a solder's rations as well as she who bore him? Women are most resourceful in providing things, and they just can't be cheated, for they know all the tricks.

------

e. PLATO: *Republic* III

No occupations belong exclusively to either men or women, but as natural abilities will be found here and there in both sexes, so women will be admitted to all pursuits on the same basis as men.

— Reading No. 12 —

PLATO'S REPUBLIC

Plato (c. 429-347) in the Republic *voiced the critical reaction of an aristocrat to the democracy of Athens, and the positive creation of an ideal commonwealth governed by genuine aristocrats, "the best people" in terms of intelligence and devotion to the public welfare.*

↗   ↗   ↗

A city is formed because men are not self-sufficient but have many wants. So each looks to others for help in supplying his various wants, and many associates and helpers come together in one place and call it a city. Everyone who gives or takes in exchange does so in the belief that he is thus serving his own best interests. It follows that more and better of everything will be produced, and more easily, when each person works at his own specialty according to his own peculiar talent, and at the proper time, without interfering with other tasks.

———

We shall tell our people the following myth. "All of you are brothers, but when you were created God mixed gold in the composition of those of you who are qualified to govern; in those fitted to be guardians he mixed silver; and in the farmers and artisans he mixed baser metals. It is therefore the first duty of our rulers to see which of these metals enters into the composition of each child that is born; and if a child of baser metal is born in the golden class they are to have no pity on it, but shall put it into the class of farmers and artisans; if, on the other hand, among that class a child of gold or silver is born, they are to raise it to its proper status. For an oracle has declared that when a city is ruled by men of baser metal it shall perish."

———

"When anyone who is by nature an artisan or other kind of producer is inflated by the wealth he has acquired or other material advantage so as to try to join the soldier-guardian class; or when a soldier tries to join the class of philosopher-rulers; or when one person attempts to be all three at one time, you will agree with me, will you not, that such changes in status and such interference will ruin the state?"

"I most certainly do agree," he said.

"This, then, is injustice. But when each of these groups —workers, soldier-guardians, and philosopher-rulers, keeps in its place and performs its own function, then justice will prevail."

———

Our object in constructing our state is not to make any one class pre-eminently happy, but to guarantee the welfare of the whole community as far as possible.

———

Unless either philosophers become rulers, or those who rule become lovers of wisdom, and so political power and philosophy are united, there can be no respite from calamity for states or for mankind.

———

Shall we not require for our rulers men who are by nature of good memory, speedy in learning, high-minded, gracious in manner, friends and brothers of truth, justice, courage, and self-control?

———

Twenty-year old youths of exceptional ability must receive special educational opportunities; the separate branches of knowledge must be developed so as to show their interrelationship and the nature of reality. At the age of thirty this group must be tested in terms of ability at dialectic, in order to discover who can advance further toward a true understanding of reality.

———

Democracy arises when the poor come to power, killing and exiling some of the opposing party, but admitting the rest to equal participation in government. Usually the officials are determined by lot. In such a city are not men free, and does not liberty of speech and action flourish, and is not every man allowed to do what he wishes? This might seem to be the most beautiful constitution of all, decorated, so to speak, with every variety of character as a dress is embroidered with every kind of flower.

———

But may we not say that democracy, like oligarchy, is destroyed by its unrestrained craving for what it considers the supreme good? In the case of oligarchy, it is wealth; in a democracy it is freedom. For excessive freedom leads to anarchy, which in turn results in despotism, the most burdensome and most brutal slavery.

———

As soon as the despot rids himself of his enemies, his first policy is to be continually starting wars so that the common people will look up to him as their necessary leader. Then he will keep them poor by taxing them to meet military expenses, and so make them less able to plot against him. And then, if he suspects anyone of being hungry for freedom, he will get rid of him; in fact, noting all those who are courageous, high-minded, sensible, and wealthy, he must of necessity be hostile to them and liquidate them. . . . The despot cannot help becoming, because of his power, more and more suspicious, untrustworthy, unjust, friendless, and depraved; he will be a most unhappy man, and make those around him as unhappy as himself.

———

A man who has joined the select company of philosophers and has come to realize how delightful and blessed is their lot, and has seen how mad the multitude is, how corrupt their politics, and how impossible for a just man to save them from folly, or his own life should he try to do so, this man will refrain from political activity and tend to his own affairs, like a traveler who finds shelter under a wall during a whirlwind. How much better it would be, however, if the

philosopher had been fortunate enough to belong to a
society which appreciated him; for then he would be
able to save the community as well as himself.

— Reading No. 13 —

ARISTOTLE'S POLITICS

*Aristotle (384-322), more interested in the classifica-
tion of existing governments than Plato, saw advantages
in various types; in order to secure stability he advocated a large and powerful middle class. The following
are excerpts from his* Politics.

All associations aim at some good, but the state, the
most lofty and inclusive of associations, aims at more
and greater good than any other. . . . When several
families become united, a village is formed; when several
villages are united in a single community, of sufficient
size to be virtually self-sufficient, the state comes into
being. Formed at the start merely to provide the neces-
sities of life, it continues for the purpose of creating the
good life. If the earlier forms of association are natural,
the state is no less so, for it is the final cause of human
association, and the nature of anything appears in its
final cause. . . . Hence it is obvious that the state is a
natural association and that man is by nature a social
and political animal. . . . Further, the state is by nature
of greater importance than the family or the individual,
since the whole is necessarily more important than the
part. . . . That the state is natural and prior to the
individual is proved by the fact that an isolated individual
is not self-sufficing. He who cannot live in society, or
does not need to because he is self-sufficient, must be
either a beast or a god; he is no member of a human

order. The gregarious instinct is a natural element in all men, and the man who first established a state was the greatest of benefactors; for man when he realizes such potentialities is the first of animals, but when he lacks law and justice he is the worst of all. . . . But justice is what binds men together in states, and the administration of justice is the first principle or order in society.

———

Governments which have concern for the common welfare are just and true forms of government, but those which concern themselves only with the interest of the rulers are inferior. . . .

We must next consider how many forms of government there are and their nature. . . . The true forms are those in which the one man, a few men, or the many, govern with the common welfare in mind; but governments which regard only private interest, whether it be of one, a few, or the many, are perverted governments. For the citizens of a state ought to share in its advantages. Of forms of government which have the common welfare in mind, when one person rules we call it monarchy; when a few rule (the best men, or at least those who have the interests of the state and the citizens at heart), aristocracy; and when the majority of the people rule in the common interest the government is called "polity.". . . The perversions of these forms are as follows: of monarchy, tyranny; of aristocracy, oligarchy; of polity, democracy. Tyranny has regard only for the interest of the ruler, oligarchy only for the interest of the wealthy, democracy only for the interest of the poor. None of them cares for the common welfare.

———

What is the best constitution for most states, and the best life for most men? It is not an ideal state which we have in mind, but a life in which the majority of people can take part and a form of government which can actually be attained. If the happy life is the life lived according to virtue, and virtue lies in a mean between extremes, the same principles apply to cities and to constitutions. Now there are three elements in all states: the very rich, the very poor, and the middle class. It is admitted that moderation and the mean are most desirable; therefore it will be best if property is possessed in moderation, for people in that situation are most inclined to act reasonably. But those who are extraordinarily handsome, strong, well-born, or wealthy find it hard to act in such a rational way. And those who are extremely poor, weak, or degraded, likewise find it hard. . . . Furthermore, the middle class is least inclined either to refuse to take part in politics or to be too ambitious for office, both of which are harmful to the community. Also people who have too much power and wealth are neither willing nor able to submit to authority. But the very poor are inferior. So the former cannot obey, and can rule only in tyrannical fashion, and the latter cannot command but must be ruled like slaves. The result is a city of masters and slaves, not of freemen; and nothing can be more deadly to states than this, for when men are hostile toward one another they refuse to travel a common road. A city should consist as far as possible of equals, and those are usually the middle classes. Therefore a city composed of middle-class citizens is made of the stoutest fabric. And these are the people who keep a city safe, for they do not, like the poor, crave their neighbor's goods, nor do others crave theirs; they neither plot against others nor are plotted against; so they pass through life in safety. It is clear, therefore, that the best community is formed by the middle class, and that those states will be well administered in which the middle class is large and stronger than both the other classes.

The argument that the majority should rule rather than the few best men might seem to have some validity. It is possible for the majority, even though each individual member is not good, to be better as a group than as individuals. When many are involved, each will have his own portion of virtue and understanding to contribute. This is why the multitude is a better judge of musical and poetic compositions; one man can judge one part, another a different part, and the whole group can judge the whole. Although each person is a worse judge than a specialist, the whole group acting together will be certainly not worse, but even better. Furthermore, sometimes the maker is not the only, or even the best, judge of his product; for example, the person who lives in a house can judge it better than the builder; a pilot can judge a rudder better than the shipwright; and one who eats the dinner, not the cook, judges the food best.

———

A man is a slave by nature when he is capable of belonging to someone else. Clearly there are some who are by nature free, others are by nature slaves, and for the latter their condition of servitude is both advantageous and just.

———

In the best-governed state the citizens must not be businessmen or manual workers, for such a life is lacking in nobility and is hostile to virtue; and they must not be farmers, since farmers lack the leisure which is necessary for the cultivation of virtue and political activity.

———

The greed of men is insatiable. The way to deal with this problem is not so much to equalize property as to persuade men of better natures not to desire more property, and prevent men of baser natures from getting more.

———

There are many disadvantages in a communistic holding of property. Our present arrangement of private property can be improved by good customs and laws so as to be better than it is now or than a communistic system. Property should be considered both common and private. When every one has the personal interest of ownership, men will have more initiative; yet, as the old proverb puts it, "Friends have things in common." This dual role of property is not impractical; it already exists in some states, where every man has private property yet makes some of it available to his friends. It is certainly better that the ownership of property should be private, but the use of it common; and it is the legislator's job to see to it that this generous state of mind is created.

———

We have now to consider the causes of revolution and how stability in government may best be secured. Revolution arises from inequality. Democracy is more secure and free from party strife than oligarchy, for in oligarchy there are two kinds of strife, that among the ruling class and that against the people, whereas in democracies the only strife that matters is that between the people and the oligarchs.

———

Democracies are overthrown chiefly because of the reckless conduct of their leaders. Sometimes these leaders arouse the wealthy to unite in opposition, sometimes they lead the people in persecuting them. (*He cites several examples of such revolutions*). For sometimes in seeking popular favor democratic leaders have made the noble class unite by treating them unfairly, either taking away their property or imposing unjust burdens on them.

———

Tyranny has the evils of both democracy and oligarchy: of oligarchy in that it aims at wealth for itself and does not trust the people; of democracy, in that it persecutes the nobles.

— Reading No. 14 —

FOREIGN RELATIONS

Herodotus (c. 440), both anthropologist and historian, was especially interested in foreign customs, which he eagerly investigated and frankly enjoyed, as did many other Greeks. But empire and war brought to Athens a

*new policy toward foreigners, devastatingly pictured by
Thucydides in his account of the subjugation of Mitylene, which sought to leave the Delian League, and the
destruction of the neutral island of Melos. Cleon, leader
of the majority party in Athens, argues for no mercy
to Mitylene; Athenian envoys try to persuade Melos to
submit.*

✓   ✓   ✓

a. HERODOTUS: *History*

In Thrace when a child is born its relatives gather
around and mourn for all the calamities it is bound to
suffer; but when a man dies they joke and rejoice at the
burial, since he has found release from his misfortunes
and has achieved happiness.

———

When Darius was king of Persia he asked the Greeks
who were there how much money they would ask for
eating their fathers' dead bodies. They replied that no
money would induce them to do it. Then he asked some
Indians, who eat their parents, what would induce them
to burn their fathers' corpses, as the Greeks do. They
replied that he should not even suggest such a horrible
thing. So firmly rooted are local customs; Pindar was
right when he said that custom is lord of all.

———

This is the most sensible custom among the Babyloni-
ans: they make no use of doctors, but instead carry a
sick person into the marketplace, where those who have
had the same illness or seen others afflicted with it come
up to him and give him advice and comfort, telling him
how they themselves got well or saw others do so.

———

Before Psammeticus was king of Egypt, the Egyptians
thought themselves to be the oldest race on earth. But
when he became king he wanted to find out what people
really were the oldest, and devised the following plan.
He took two new-born children of plain people and gave
them to a shepherd to bring up among his sheep, in-

structing him that no one should say a word near them. He ordered this because he wanted to hear what sort of words the children would say when they started to talk. And the experiment succeeded. For after the shepherd had done as he was ordered for two years, one day as he entered the fold the children ran toward him, hands outstretched, calling "Bekos." After this had occurred several times the shepherd brought the children before the king so that Psammeticus could hear the words himself. Then the king sought to find out what people used the word Bekos, and discovered it was a Phrygian word for bread. From this the Egyptians concluded that the Phrygians were an older race than they. This account was told by priests in the temple of Hephaestus (Ptah) at Memphis.

———

Croesus said to Cyrus, "No man is such a fool as to desire war instead of peace; for in peace sons bury their fathers, but in war fathers bury their sons."

———

b. THUCYDIDES: *History* III

CLEON. I have often realized that a democracy is incompetent to control an empire, but never more than today, when I see you having a change of heart about punishing the people of Mitylene. You must remember that your empire is a despotism imposed on intriguing subjects, who are ruled against their will, and who obey you, not because of any kindness you do them or any good will they feel toward you, but only in so far as you are stronger than they are and impose your will on them.

Most important of all, we must stop everlastingly changing our minds, and realize that a state with inferior laws which are enforced is better off than one whose laws are good but ineffective.

So I maintain you should not reverse your former decision to punish them, or be misled by pity, delight in clever arguments, or mercy—three things most prejudicial to empire. I will sum it up briefly: If you take my advice you will do what is just to the people of

Mitylene and what is expedient for us; but if you decide otherwise you will not be thanked by them but rather condemned. For if these people had a right to revolt, then you are wrong in exercising imperial power. But if, rightly or wrongly, you are determined to rule, then you must punish these people, justly or not in your own interest. If you fail to do so you must give up your empire, and then you can practice your virtues to your heart's content. I say punish them as we formerly decided. Pay them back for the trouble they have caused. Stop being tender-hearted. Remember the danger that we lately faced, and by punishing the people of Mitylene warn your other allies that whoever revolts shall perish.

----

c. THUCYDIDES: *History* V

ATHENIANS. We shall not make a long and tiresome speech about how we deserve our power because we defeated Persia, or that we have suffered some injury at your hands. Similarly we ask you not to try to convince us that you should not join us because you were originally colonized by Sparta, or because you have never done us any harm.

Let both of us be sensible and say what we really intend, since you know as well as we do that justice is arrived at by deliberation only when the two sides are equal, and that the strong exact all they can and the weak yield what they must.

MELIANS. You say we must ignore justice and deal merely with what is expedient, but we believe you will find it expedient not to rule out an appeal to reason and justice, because if you should be ultimately defeated your enemies would judge you by your own example.

ATHENIANS. What may happen to our empire is our own affair. We are here now to act to the advantage of our empire, and what we propose is also to your advantage; for if you submit without fighting it will be easier for us, and you will avoid complete ruin.

MELIANS. We realize how weak in power we are. But we have faith that the gods will help us in this contest between justice and injustice.

ATHENIANS. We expect to have the favor of the gods
quite as much as you, for as far as the gods are concerned we believe, as of men we know, that by a necessity of their nature they rule wherever they have the
power to do so. We did not invent this principle, nor
are we the first to act upon it. We found it already
existing, and we expect people in the future will continue
to use it. You and others, if you had the power we have,
would do what we are doing.

— Reading No. 15 —

THE MAN OF COURAGE

*The love of freedom and the courage to die in pre-
serving freedom for one's country were commemorated
in many grave inscriptions written by Simonides, in
Herodotus' accounts of Tellus of Athens and of the over-
throw of the tyrants, and in the battle-cry of the Athenian sailors as their ships advanced against the Persian
armada at Salamis (480 B.C.), as reported in Aeschylus'*
Persians. *But there is another courage: the will to fight
for individual freedom of thought and action, represented
by Socrates in his speech when on trial, as reported by
Plato in the* Apology.

✓   ✓   ✓

a. SIMONIDES

Stranger passing by, tell the Spartans that we lie
here, having done what they told us to do. (*On the
Spartan dead at Thermopylae*).

If to die nobly is the greatest mark of virtue, to us
of all men Fortune gave this prize. For eager to crown
Greece with freedom, here we lie enjoying ageless glory.
(*On the Athenian dead at Plataea*).

b. HERODOTUS: *History* I

CROESUS. Whom do you, Solon, consider the happiest man you have known?

SOLON. Tellus of Athens. To begin with, his city was prosperous. He had a family of attractive and responsible sons, who in turn had children, all of whom survived. He had enough means to live comfortably, according to our modest standards. Finally, he met death nobly, for in a battle between the Athenians and the people of Eleusis, he came to the rescue of his countrymen and helped rout the enemy before he fell; and the Athenians gave him a state funeral with a hero's honors.

c. HERODOTUS: *History* VIII

The power of Athens increased. And here is proof that freedom is a good thing, for when the Athenians were under a tyrant they were no better soldiers than their neighbors, but when they got rid of tyrants they were far superior. Clearly they did not work hard while in subjection, because they were working for a master; but when they became free, each person was eager to work because he profited from his labor.

d. AESCHYLUS: *Persians*

On, sons of Hellas, free your fatherland, free your children, your wives, the shrines of your ancestral gods, the tombs of your forefathers. Now everything we love is at stake.

e. PLATO: *Apology*

SOCRATES. Some one of you may ask, "What have you been doing, Socrates, to have caused such charges to be brought against you? Certainly you must have done something unusual. Tell us, so that we may not condemn you wrongly." That is a reasonable request, and I shall try to explain what has caused this slander. A sort of wisdom which I possess is responsible for my reputation; and for that wisdom I shall give as a reference an authority in whom you believe: Apollo, the god of Delphi.

You knew Chaerephon, and you know how enthusiastic he was in everything he undertook. Well, he went to Delphi and asked the oracle if there was anyone wiser than I; and Apollo answered that there was no one wiser. When I heard of it I said to myself, "What can he mean by this riddle? I know that I am not wise in any respect. What does he mean by saying that I am the wisest of men? He is a god, so he cannot lie." For a long time I was baffled. Then I decided to go to one of the men considered to be wise, and disprove the oracle, saying to Apollo, "Here is a man wiser than I, but you said I was the wisest." After observing him and conversing with him (I won't say who he was, but he was a political leader), I concluded that he seemed to other men, and most of all to himself, to be wise, but actually he was not wise. Then I tried to point this out to him, but merely caused myself to be hated by him and by many others who were present. So I said to myself, "I am certainly wiser than he is. Probably neither of us knows anything of real value; but he thinks he knows when he doesn't, whereas I am aware of my ignorance. In this respect perhaps I am wiser than he." (*After this Socrates went to other prominent men in the community, including poets and expert craftsmen, and discovered that they, too, had the reputation of being wise but failed to realize the significance of what they did.*) As a result of this inquiry many people have come to regard me with violent hostility, and many slanders have been directed against me. And people call me wise, for they imagine that I have the wisdom which I reveal as lacking in others. But really, men of Athens, only God is wise; and by his oracular response he indicates that human wisdom is worth little or nothing, and that the wisest man is the one who, like Socrates, knows how slight his wisdom is. And I shall not cease questioning and cross-examining anyone I meet, be he citizen or foreigner, who seems to be wise; and if I find he is not, I shall reveal to him his ignorance.

———

But perhaps some one will say, "Aren't you ashamed, Socrates, of behaving in such a way that now you may be put to death for it?" Here is my answer. "You are wrong about that. A man who is worth anything should not calculate the chance of living or dying, but should consider only whether he is doing the right or the wrong thing and behaving like a good man or a bad one. For wherever a man's place is, whether one of his own choice or one in which he has been stationed by a commanding officer in battle, there he should remain in the time of danger, and should give no thought to death. It would be strange, men of Athens, if, when I had been given orders by our generals at Potidaea, Amphipolis, and Delium, I had stayed where they put me, but now when, as I believe, God has commanded me to enquire critically into myself and other men, I were to leave my post through fear of death or anything else. That certainly would be strange, and then I might with justice be brought to trial for denying that the gods exist, if I so disobeyed the god's will because I feared death and imagined I was wise when I was not. For to fear death is to pretend one knows what one does not know. No one knows whether death, which men fear as the greatest of evils, may not be the greatest good. In this respect alone perhaps I am wiser than other men: knowing little about what happens after death I do not pretend I know. But I do know this: that injustice and disobedience to what is better, whether divine or human, is evil and dishonorable; and I shall never fear or avoid a possible good more than a certain evil.

So if you release me now, and say to me, "Socrates, this time we'll let you off, but on this condition: that you will not engage in such criticism any more. If we catch you doing so again you shall die"—if you said that, I would answer: "Men of Athens, I honor and love you, but I shall obey God rather than you, and while I live and have the strength to do it I shall continue my pursuit of understanding, saying to anyone whom I meet, 'You, my friend, a citizen of the great and powerful and intellectual city of Athens, aren't you ashamed of amassing as much wealth and prestige as you can but paying so little if any attention to understanding the truth and your soul's progress?' And if the man protests and says he does care, I do not let him get off so easily, but I question and cross-examine him; and if I think he has no goodness in him but only says he has, I upbraid him for his false set of values. And I shall keep on doing this with everyone whom I meet, for you must realize that this is my assignment from God, and I believe no greater good has ever happened in our city than this service of mine."

———

Upon reflection we shall see that we are justified in hoping that death is a good thing. For it is either a state of unconsciousness, or, according to what men say, it is a change of form and residence for the soul from this world to another. Now if it is total unconsciousness, then death is a gain, for eternity is just one long night. But if it is a journey to another place where, as they say, all the dead reside, what could be a greater good than that? What wouldn't a man give for the opportunity to talk with Orpheus and Musaeus, Hesiod and Homer? Futhermore, I can continue my investigation into knowledge. And there they do not put a man to death for asking questions! So, my judges, be cheerful about death, and be sure that no harm can come to a good man either living or dead.

— Reading No. 16 —

THE RATIONAL MAN

In the "hymn of humanism" in Sophocles' Antigone, the chorus praises the achievements made by man's intelligence. Socrates through a process of questioning tried to develop the faculty of reason in his youthful followers and guide them toward sound definitions; the Lysis and Meno present this procedure in its simpler terms. Plato, using the Socratic method, analyzed the construction of general concepts and the process of understanding. Aristotle made a systematic study of ideas in their logical relationships and social contexts.

✓   ✓   ✓

a. SOPHOCLES: *Antigone*

There are many wonderful things, but none more wonderful than man. Over the whitecaps of the sea he goes, driven by the stormy winds, topped by the towering waves; and the Earth, oldest of the gods, eternal and tireless, he wears away, turning furrows with his plough year after year. He snares the lighthearted birds and the wild beasts of the fields, and he catches in his nets the fish of the sea, man forever resourceful. He tames the animals that roam the meadows and mountains, yoking the shaggy horses and the powerful bulls. And he has learned the use of language to express windswift thought, and he has mastered the art of living with other men in addition to the conquest of nature. Skillfully he meets the future; although he has found no escape from death, he has discovered release from painful diseases. His ingenuity results in evil as well as good; when he respects his country's laws and justice he deserves honor; but may the arrogant man, untrue to his city, never come to my hearth or share my thoughts.

---

b. PLATO ON SOCRATES: *Lysis* and *Meno*

I suppose, Lysis, your father and mother love you very much?

Of course, Socrates.

Then they would wish you to be as happy as possible. Why not?

Does a person seem to you happy when he is a slave and cannot do what he wants to?

By Zeus, I wouldn't say so.

So if your father and mother love you and want you to be happy they obviously put themselves out in order to please you?

Why not?

So they let you do what you wish, and they don't punish you or prevent you from doing anything you set your heart on?

Oh but they do prevent my doing very many things, Socrates.

What's that? They want you to be happy yet prevent you from doing what you wish? Let's say you want to ride on one of your father's chariots and take the reins when he is competing in a race, wouldn't they let you do it?

By Zeus they wouldn't.

Whom do they let do it?

Oh there's a charioteer, and father pays him to do it.

You mean to say they let a hired man do whatever he wishes with the horses, but they won't let you?

Certainly.

Well, tell me this. Do they let you govern yourself, or don't they let you do that, either?

Of course not!

Who does govern you?

This pedagogue (*attendant*) here.

Is he a slave?

Of course, but he belongs to us.

It's a terrible thing for a free man to be governed by a slave. Just what does he do in ordering you around?

He takes me to my teacher's school.

And these teachers also give orders to you?

They certainly do.

Well, your father certainly has put a great many masters over you. But when you go home to your mother, I'm sure she lets you do whatever you wish, so that you'll be her happy boy.

(*Lysis proceeds to explain that his mother also prevents him from interfering in her household tasks. "Why don't they let you do what you want?" Socrates asks. The boy answers, "Because I am not yet old enough." But then Socrates gets him to admit that his father and mother allow him to do many things, such as reading and writing, as he wishes. Lysis works out a new definition: "They let me do what I understand how to do, and prevent me from doing things which I don't understand." The implied conclusion is that people are happy when they do what they can do well, and should not expect to be allowed to do things of which they are ignorant. There is also implied a criticism of the extreme democratic dogma of individual liberty.*)

Do we call virtue a good thing, Meno?

Yes, Socrates.

Well, if any good exists apart from knowledge, that good might be virtue; but if knowledge includes all good, then we are correct in considering virtue to be knowledge?

Right.

Virtue makes us good?

Yes.

And good things profit us?

Certainly.

Then virtue profits us?

Obviously.

Now let us examine what special things profit us. Health? Strength? Beauty? Wealth?

Yes.

And yet these same things may at times harm us, may they not?

Yes.

What determines whether they are profitable or not? Don't they profit us when they are properly used, and harm us when they are improperly used?

Right.

Now let us examine spiritual goods, such as self-control, justice, courage, keenness of mind, memory, generosity and so forth. These, too, sometimes profit and sometimes harm us; for example when a man lacks good sense he may be harmed by courage.

Quite true.

If, then, virtue is a quality of the soul and is profitable, it must be wisdom, or at least common-sense, since none of the other qualities of the soul is in itself either profitable or harmful, but is made so by wisdom or folly. Similarly with the other goods we mentioned, such as wealth.

Yes.

Is not this universally true, that all good things depend on the soul, and the qualities of the soul depend upon wisdom?

Yes.

But if virtue is knowledge, it may be taught. And I sometimes doubt whether it can be taught, for I have gone to great efforts to find teachers of it and have never succeeded in finding any.

C. PLATO

The good man does not let any element in his soul usurp the function of another, but like a musician who brings into harmony all the musical tones, so the good man, relating perfectly the three elements within himself (appetite, unselfish spirit, reason) becomes harmonious. (*Republic* IV)

A musical education is of the greatest importance, because rhythm and harmony penetrate very deeply to the inward places of the soul and affect it most powerfully, imparting grace; and also because one who has been so educated will perceive most keenly the defects of both art and nature. With fine discrimination he will approve and enjoy beautiful objects, and thus grow himself to be beautiful and good. But shameful things he will censure and hate, even in his youth before he is able to understand the reason why; and when reason comes he will recognize and welcome her in the most friendly way because of this early training. (*Republic* III)

Poets should be compelled to express in their productions the likeness of a good character, and other artists must be restrained from expressing an evil nature, intemperance, meanness, and ungracefulness, whether in the likeness of living creatures, or buildings, or any other craftsmanship. He who cannot do otherwise shall be forbidden to work in our city, so that our guardians may not be reared among images of evil, as upon unwholesome pastures. We ought rather to seek artists who desire to track down what is beautiful and graceful, so that our youth, living in a healthful climate, may derive good from every side, whence any emanation from beautiful works may strike upon their sight like a breeze wafting health from kindly lands, and from childhood win them into resemblance, friendship, and harmony with intellectual beauty. (*Republic* III)

He who is eager to love rightly should begin when he is young to seek the companionship of beautiful objects; and first he should learn to love one such object only, and out of that to create beautiful thoughts. Soon he will realize that the beauty of any one object is closely related to the beauty of another, and then, if beauty of form is his pursuit, he will be very foolish not to recognize that the beauty in all objects is one and the same thing. When he perceives this he will become a lover of all beautiful objects. Next he will consider that the beauty of the soul is more excellent than the beauty of the outward form, and will be led to see the beauty of institutions and laws, and after that of the various fields of knowledge. Then no longer will he meanly and unreasonably enslave himself to the attractions of any one person or institution, but drawing near the wide sea of beauty he will grow in understanding, until at last, strong and mature, he contemplates one comprehensive science, the science of universal beauty. (*Symposium*)

There is a kind of madness which inspires a man who, when he sees the beauty of this earth, remembers with ecstasy the true Beauty. And this is of all inspirations the best. For every man's soul has, by its nature, formerly contemplated reality, but to remember it is no easy matter; there are only a few who, when they see the objects of earth, are reminded by them of the realities. Once, with the rest of the happy band, we saw radiant beauty, we beheld the beatific vision, we were initiated into mysteries which it is right to call most blessed. We were admitted to the sight of visions perfect and complete and serene and happy, shining in pure light. There beauty shone with the rest; and when we came to earth we found her here, too, shining clearly, through the medium of sight, our clearest sense. (*Phaedrus*)

------

d. ARISTOTLE

Every art, investigation, and activity is thought to aim at some good, so the good has been properly defined as the end toward which everything aims. . . . If there is such an end, will not knowing it be of great value to us? Shall we not, like bowmen with a mark to shoot at, be more likely to hit upon what is right? . . . To say that happiness is the chief good may seem a commonplace. A more precise definition of it is desirable. Perhaps we can arrive at it if we first consider the nature of man. For just as for a flute player, a sculptor, or any artist, in fact for everything that has a function, the good is regarded as residing in the function, so with man, if he has a special function. . . . What can that function be? Not merely life, for life is common even to vegetation, so we may exclude the experience of nutrition and growth. Perception? No, for that is common to animals. There remains the active experience of the rational faculty. . . . Now if the function of man is an activity of the soul in accordance with a rational principle, human good is an activity of the soul in accordance with virtue, and if there are several virtues, in accordance with the best and most complete virtue.

But to this we must add "in a complete life." For as one swallow on a single fine day does not make the summer, so a single day or short period of time does not make a man really happy. . . . And happiness also requires external goods; for it is, if not impossible, at least difficult to act nobly without suitable possessions. In many activities we need to make use of friends, wealth, and political power. And happiness is lessened if one lacks good birth, fine children, personal beauty; for a man who is very ugly or low-born or alone and childless is not apt to be very happy.

———

Since happiness is an activity of the soul in accordance with perfect virtue, we must next consider the nature of virtue. . . . Some of the virtues are intellectual in character, others are moral; philosophic wisdom and insight and wisdom of a practical sort are intellectual, generosity and temperance are moral. . . . Intellectual virtue owes in general both its existence and growth to teaching, while moral virtue results from habit. . . . It is obvious that none of the moral virtues is inherent in us, for nothing that exists by nature can form a habit contrary to its nature. For example, a stone which naturally falls downward cannot be made to move itself upward even if one tries to train it to do so by throwing it up countless times. . . . Nature merely makes us able to receive such virtues, which are perfected by habit.

If happiness is activity in accordance with the highest virtue, this virtue will be the best of our faculties—either reason, or something else in us which rules and guides us, which makes us think of noble and divine things. . . . For man, living in accordance with reason seems best, since the function of man is essentially the exercise of reason.

———

We acquire virtues by exercising them, as is true of any art. We learn by doing. As men become carpenters by building houses and lyre players by playing the lyre, we become just by acting justly, moderate by doing things in moderation, courageous by showing courage. Further evidence is seen in the experience of cities; legislators habituate the citizens to civic virtue.

———

Virtue is a condition of character involving choice and lying in a mean, the mean being determined by the rational principle which a man of practical wisdom would make use of. It is a mean between two evils, one of which is of excess, the other of defect. . . . As far as fear and overconfidence are concerned, courage is the mean. . . . As far as giving and taking money is concerned, the mean is generosity, whereas the excess is prodigality and the defect is stinginess. . . . As far as honor and dishonor are concerned, the mean is legitimate pride, whereas the excess is vanity and the defect is self-abasement. . . .

———

Justice is the proportional, and injustice is contrary to the proper proportion. The man who acts unjustly has too much of a good thing; the man unjustly treated has too little of it.

———

Not every type of experience, however, admits a mean. Some are essentially bad; such attitudes as malice, shamelessness, and jealousy, and such actions as adultery, theft, and murder. . . . To achieve the mean is often not easy. How, for instance, should one be angry, at whom, under what circumstances, for how long? It is nonetheless clear that the effort to attain the mean is praiseworthy.

Friendship is a most necessary virtue, for no one would want to live without friends, even if he had every other possession. Men of wealth and political office especially need friends, for of what avail is their prosperity if they have no chance to use it in praiseworthy generosity toward friends? How, in fact, can prosperity be protected without friends? And in poverty and other disasters friends often seem one's sole refuge. . . . But in addition to being necessary, friendship is a noble thing; we commend those who have many friends and love them.

Perfect happiness consists in the activity of contemplation. (*Nicomachean Ethics*)

Obviously people in the prime of life will be intermediate between the young and the old. They will not be subject to the excess of either. They will be neither foolhardy nor excessively cautious, but will preserve a good balance of confidence and fear. They will be neither overtrustful nor generally distrustful, but will come to conclusions on the basis of the facts. They will govern their conduct by motives of neither prestige nor expediency alone, but by both, and they will preserve the mean between stinginess and extravagance. Similarly with passion and desire: they will combine temperance and vital spirit, whereas the young are brave and intemperate, and the old are temperate but overcautious. In conclusion it may be claimed that the separate advantages of youth and age are both enjoyed by men in the prime of life, and the disadvantages of excess or defect common to youth and age are avoided by men in the prime of life, which is physically from the ages of 30 to 35, mentally about the age of 49. (*Rhetoric*)

Tragedy is an artistic representation of experience that is serious, complete (*i.e.*, the tragic error leading to the tragic conclusion), and of adequate magnitude; it is acted, not merely recited; it is expressed in speech made beautiful in various suitable ways; and its purpose is to arouse pity and fear and purge the spectator of such emotions.

In tragedy of the highest type the plot must represent experience which arouses pity and fear. There are, therefore, three kinds of plot to be avoided: (1) a good man must not be shown proceeding from happiness to misery; or (2) a bad man from misery to happiness. In the first case we are not aroused to fear or pity, but find the situation intolerable; in the second, there is no appeal to any sympathetic feeling in us. Nor (3) should an exceptionally bad man be shown proceeding from happiness to misery. That sort of account may arouse some sort of feeling in us, but it will not be pity or fear. Pity is aroused by undeserved calamity; fear is aroused by the calamity of some one essentially like ourselves. There remains, therefore, the man in an intermediate position, neither extraordinarily good and just nor vile and depraved, whose calamity is brought about by some error on his part. (*Poetics*)

— Reading No. 17 —

TRAGEDY: EURIPIDES' *MEDEA*

The Medea *of Euripides, produced in Athens in 431, is an example of the tragic effect of pity and fear described by Aristotle and of other values in Greek drama.*

In the following scene Medea's children return after having carried to the Princess the poisoned gifts which are Medea's revenge on the girl who has taken her husband from her. For the sake of her children Medea believes that she must now kill them.

↗   ↗   ↗

(*Enter Attendant and Children.*)

ATTENDANT. Mistress, the children have won release from exile! And the royal bride was delighted with your gifts! Now all's fair sailing for the children!

But what's this? Why do you stand there as if all were lost when you have succeeded so well? Why aren't you glad when you hear the news I bring?

MEDEA. O God!

ATTENDANT. This isn't the way to hear good news.

MEDEA. God!

ATTENDANT. Can it be that I've brought bad fortune without knowing it? Shall I get no credit for bringing good news?

MEDEA. You have reported what you reported. I don't blame you.

ATTENDANT. Then why is your face downcast? Why weep?

MEDEA. I have great reason, old man. For the gods and I have planned and done a terrible thing.

ATTENDANT. Courage! Your children shall one day bring you back home.

MEDEA. I shall bring them home before that.

ATTENDANT. You're not the only woman who has lost her children. Mortals must learn to be reconciled to misfortune.

MEDEA. I shall learn it. But go inside now and arrange things for the boys.

(*The Attendant goes in*)

O children, children, for you there is a city and a home in which, without your wretched mother, you will live forever. But I am going to another country for refuge before I am of any further help to you, before I see you happily grown up, before I make arrangements for your weddings—the marriage bath, the bed, the torches, the bride. What agony my ambition has brought me! It was not for this, children, that I labored and was wracked with pain when you were born; it was not for this I brought you up. Oh no, once I had great hopes in you, that you would comfort me in my old age and when I died would lay me out tenderly with your own hands. What woman doesn't yearn for that? But now I have no such lovely dream. Without you I shall lead a bitter life and a hopeless one. And you shall never again look on your mother with those dear eyes, but will be living in an alien land.

O God, why do you look at me so, children? Why do you laugh that last laughter?

What am I about? My courage has left me, women, when I see my children's shining faces. I can never do it. I abandon the plan I had. I shall take my children with me. To make their father suffer why must I suffer twice as much as he? No, I won't do it. Farewell to my whole plan.

And yet, what am I dreaming of? Do I want to become a laughing stock to my enemies by letting them go unpunished? This must be dared! Away with my cowardice and the tender thoughts that undermine my resolution. Go into the house, children.

(*The children slowly go in.*)

Whoever is forbidden to attend my sacrifice, let him beware. I shall not let my hand swerve.

O my soul, do not do it! Let them live, wretched Medea, spare your sons! If they live with you in Athens they will give you joy.

No, by the avenging spirits of Hades, I shall never let my sons be handed to my foes to gloat over. There is no way out of it, they must die. And since they must die, I, who gave them birth, shall kill them. There is no way to evade it. Already the diadem is on the princess' head, the bride is being eaten by that robe of poison, I know it well. But before I walk the path of utter misery, I must speak again to my sons.

(*A servant brings them out to her.*)

Give mother your hands, children. O dearest hands, dearest lips and bodies, princely faces! May you be happy! But there, not here! Your father took away any happiness you could have here. O lovely look, O soft flesh and sweetest breath of my children—Go in the house! Go!

(*The servant takes them in.*)

I can no longer look at them; I am overcome by my woe. Now I realize what a terrible thing I am going to do. But I have more passion than reason, even though I know what disaster passion brings.

CHORUS OF CORINTHIAN WOMEN.

Often have I debated keenly about life
And struggled to resolve its many mysteries
More than women are credited with doing.
For there is the gift of speculation
Even among women, the craving to understand,
Not among all, only a few of them,
You might find one in a great number,
But women, too, are lovers of wisdom.

And I conclude that those among mortals
Who are childless have the best fortune.
For being childless and unaware
Whether their loss is woe or joy,
They live free from many a pain.
But those who have within their homes
The fragrant flower of tender youth
Are burdened all their days with care.

First to rear them properly,
And then to leave them means to live.
Never sure if all their toil
Is for good or worthless sons.
And then there comes a final fear—
They have found wealth to rear the young,
The bodies have grown to manhood, the mind
Noble—but if a god decrees,

Death comes. Down to the dark of Hades
He takes the bodies of your sons.
How then profits a man, having suffered
All else, to have this pain the more,
The sharpest pang given by the gods,
The bitterest grief imposed on men?

MEDEA. Friends, I have waited a long time for this to happen, and I am expecting now the report of it. I see one of Jason's servants approaching. From his labored breathing he shows what sort of news he brings.

(*Enter Messenger.*)

MESSENGER. You who have done this criminal thing, Medea, escape, escape, by any means you can, ship on the sea or waggon rolling over the earth!

MEDEA. What has happened that should force me to escape?

MESSENGER. The Royal Princess is dead, and Creon her father, slain by your poison.

MEDEA. That's wonderful news. Hereafter you shall be counted among my benefactors and friends.

MESSENGER. What? Are you sane and in your right mind, to do such injury to royalty and then rejoice when you hear about it? Aren't you afraid?

MEDEA. I shall have something to say to that later. But now take your time, my friend, and tell me how they died. You will make me twice as happy if they died horribly.

MESSENGER. When your two children came with their father to the bride's apartment we were delighted, we servants who shared your troubles. The rumor spread through the palace that you and your husband had become reconciled, and one of us would kiss the hand, another the golden hair of your children, and as for me, in my happiness I followed them even to the women's quarters.

The mistress whom we now pay homage to instead of you did not see the children at first, but was all eagerness when she saw Jason coming in. Then when she caught sight of the children, she was disgusted and half closed her eyes and turned her head away, but your husband soothed her and calmed her by saying, "Don't be unkind to those who love you. Stop being angry; just look at them and treat those who are dear to your husband as dear to you, too. Take these gifts they bring, and persuade your father to let them stay here for my sake, won't you?" And she, when she saw the box of finery, did not hold back any longer, but granted her husband all he asked.

When the children and their father had just left the room she took out the embroidered dress and tried it on, and fastened the golden diadem about her head, fixed her hair before a gleaming mirror, and laughed gaily at the image—already as good as dead—that she saw there. Then she got up from her seat and walked to and fro, treading delicately across the room with white feet flashing. How happy she was over those presents! Often she would look over her shoulder to see how the train fell. . . .

But all of a sudden a sickening change took place. She became deathly pale, she staggered sideways, her legs started to tremble, and she just managed to sink into a chair to avoid falling on the floor. One of the old servants thought she fainted through emotion sent by Pan or some other god, and gave a cry of holy rejoicing—until she saw the white foam oozing on the princess' lips, and her eyeballs twisted upward, and her face drained of its color. Then she raised a cry of another sort, a piercing cry of pity. One servant ran to the King's apartment, another to the bridegroom's, to let them know of the bride's illness, and the whole palace resounded with people running.

It was about as long as it takes a swift walker to cover the stadium course before she recovered her speech and opened her eyes and began to moan terribly. Then she wrenched herself up, poor woman, and entered the field against two merciless foes. The golden diadem which encircled her head sent forth a terrifying stream of devouring fire, and the delicate dress—those gifts your children brought her—began to eat away her white flesh. She leaped to her feet and ran all ablaze, shaking her hair and head, trying to throw off the diadem, but the golden clasp held firm, and the fire, as she shook her head, blazed twice as fiercely. She fell on the threshold, no match for her doom, hardly recognizable by anyone except her father. For her eyes were nearly gone, her face eaten away, blood dripped from the top of her head, clotted with fire, and the flesh was oozing from her bones like resin from a pine tree. Such jaws your secret poison had! She was a horrible sight. Everyone was afraid to touch her dead body, for we had seen enough to teach us better.

But her father, poor man, not knowing what had happened, suddenly appeared in the room and fell on the corpse, moaning and folding his arms around her and kissing her. "My poor child," he kept saying, "What god has ruined you so cruelly? Who has brought me to death by robbing me of you? I wish I could die with you, my daughter." At last he stopped his moaning and tried to raise his old body, but he was held as ivy clings to laurel branches. The delicate dress clung to him, and gave him a fiendish wrestling match. When he wanted to lift a knee, the cloth gripped it, and if he wrenched it away the aged flesh was stripped from his bones. Finally he gave up, the ill-fated King, and he breathed his last, for he was no longer able to struggle with his doom. There they lie together, a sight for tears, the bodies of the girl and the old father.

As far as I am concerned—what will happen to you is your own affair; you will perhaps know how to find a refuge from punishment—I have always thought that mortal life is only a shadow and that men who seem wise and subtle of speech pay the greatest penalty. No man, in fact, is truly happy. In prosperity one man might be luckier than another; that's all you can say.

CHORUS LEADER. It seems as if some divinity has heaped up woe for Jason on this day, and rightly so. O poor princess, how we pity you, who go to Hades because of having married Jason.

MEDEA. Friends, my mind is made up to kill my children at once, and then escape from this land. I must not by any delay let my sons be seized and murdered by a crueler hand than mine. This must be; there is no escape. And since it must be, I who bore them shall kill them. Come my heart, steel yourself. Why do I delay doing the terrible thing that must be done? Come wretched hand, take the dagger, take it, run the tragic race of pain, never flinch, never remember they are your children, how unspeakably dear they are, how you bore them—forget for this one short day that they are your children. Then for the rest of your life you can grieve for them. And grieving will be easy, for even if you kill them they were dear to you, and no woman is so miserable as I.

(*Medea goes into the house.*)

STOICS

The Hymn to Zeus *by Cleanthes (331-232) is an eloquent statement of the Stoic faith. The leading Stoic writer on ethics was Epictetus, a slave at Rome during the reign of Nero.*

1   1   1

a. CLEANTHES: *Hymn to Zeus*

Most glorious and omnipotent Zeus, ruler of Nature, worshipped under many names, by whom all things are governed in accordance with Law, hail to thee! From thee we are born, and alone of all living things on the earth are created in the likeness of God. So I shall forever praise thy power, by which the heaven is moved and directed in its course around the earth, rejoicing in thy control. For thou hast as thy servant in thy victorious hands heaven's double-edged thunderbolt of imperishable fire, pulsing its way through every creature which obeys thee; and with it thou dost direct Universal Reason which moves through all creation, mingling with the sun and with the hosts of stars. All things on earth, in the sea, or in the air above confess thee as their author, except the deeds of evil and foolish men; but even such discords thou knowest how to weave into a total harmony, making what is disorderly orderly, what is hostile friendly, in accordance with the Law of Reason which blind men cannot understand. Instead they suffer loss when they seek happiness in their own fashion, knowing not the Divine Law. Some of them pursue prestige, some wealth, some sensual delight. Fools they are, who strive in vain. But do thou, Zeus, giver of all, cloud-gatherer and lord of the lightning, save men from their bitter ignorance, dispel their sorrow and grief, and grant them wisdom, for by wisdom thou dost rule with power and justice. In return for thy blessing we give thee and thy work our everlasting praise. And there is no greater glory for men or for gods than to praise forever Universal Reason.

---

b. EPICTETUS: *Discourses*

The man is free whom nothing hinders, who deals with things as he wishes. But the man who can be hindered or driven into anything against his will is a slave. And who lives without hindrance? He who aims at nothing which is not his own. And what things are not our own? Whatever we are powerless to have or not to have, or to have of a certain quality or under certain conditions. The body, then, is not our own; property is not our own. If you crave one of these things as if it were your own, you will pay the price merited by the man who desires what is not his. The road leading to freedom, the only release from slavery, is to be able to say cheerfully

> Lead me on, O Zeus and Destiny,
> Where I was once assigned by Thy decree.

Man has been brought into the world to be a spectator of God and his works, and not only a spectator but also an interpreter. So it is shameful for man to begin and end where irrational animals do; rather he should begin like them but end where nature has ended concerning us; and nature ended with contemplation and understanding and a way of life harmonious with her. See to it, therefore, that you do not die before witnessing these things. You take a trip to Olympia to see the statue by Phidias, and each of you thinks it a misfortune to die before seeing such sights; but when there is no need of journeying, when God is already present in his works, will you not desire to see those works and understand them? Will you not perceive who you are, for what you were born, and what this purpose is for which you have received your sight?

"But there are disagreeable and difficult things in life."

Aren't there also in Olympia? Don't you suffer from the heat? Aren't you crammed into crowded seats? Don't

you have trouble in getting a bath? Aren't you drenched
when it rains? Don't you have the dubious advantage of
tumult and shouting and other discomforts? But I imagine you endure and put up with all these things, so
unimportant are they compared with the glory of the
spectacle. Come now, haven't you received faculties
which enable you to endure every happening? Haven't
you courage? And what concern of mine is anything
that happens if I am magnanimous? What shall upset
me or confound me or seem to me painful?

Anyone who has carefully studied the administration
of the universe and has learned that "the greatest and
most powerful and most comprehensive of all governments is this one which is composed of men and God,
and that from God have come the seeds of existence to
all things begotten and growing on the earth, and most
of all to rational creatures, since they alone by nature
share in the society of God, woven together with him
through the faculty of reason"—why will not such a
man call himself a citizen of the universe, a son of God,
and why shall he fear anything that happens among men?

What language is adequate to praise all the works of
Providence in us or to give them their proper place?
If we were intelligent ought we do anything else but
publicly and in private to hymn and magnify God and
tell of His grace to us? Ought we not while digging and
ploughing and eating to sing this hymn to God? "Great
is God, who has given us these instruments wherewith
we shall work the earth. Great is God, who has given
us hands, the ability to swallow food, a belly, the power
to grow without conscious effort, and to breath while
sleeping." This we should sing in every situation, and in
addition the greatest and most divine hymn, that God has
given us the faculty to understand these things and follow the road of Reason. What then? Since most of you
have become blind, should not some one fulfill this duty
for you, singing on behalf of all this hymn to God? What

else can I, a lame old man, do but sing God's praise?
If I were a nightingale I would sing as a nightingale; if
I were a swan, I would sing as a swan. But, being a
rational man, I must sing God's praise. This is my task;
I do it, I shall not desert this post as long as it is assigned to me, and I exhort you to sing with me this
same song.

— Reading No. 19 —

EPICURUS

*Founding their philosophy on the teachings of Epi-
curus (342-270) of Athens, the Epicureans adopted
atomistic materialism in their cosmology, and denied that
there was any interference of the gods in human affairs
or any existence for men after death. The following
excerpts are from Epicurus'* Golden Maxims, *preserved
in Diogenes Laertius'* Lives of Eminent Philosophers.

Pleasure is an original and natural good, but we do
not choose every pleasure. Sometimes we eschew pleasures when a greater pain follows them; and many pains
we consider preferable to pleasure when they lead eventually to a greater pleasure. Self-sufficiency is to be
sought. Luxuries are hard to get, but natural things are
easy and give us much pleasure.

When we say that pleasure is the purpose of life, we
do not mean the pleasures of the sensually self-indulgent,
as some assert, but rather freedom from bodily pain
and mental disturbance. The life of pleasure does not
come from drinking or revels, or other sensual pleasures.

It comes from sober thinking, the sensible investigation of what to choose and to avoid, and getting rid of ideas which agitate the soul. Common sense is our best guide. It tells us that we cannot live happily unless we live wisely, nobly, and justly; nor can we live wisely, nobly, and justly without being happy. The virtues are inseparably linked with pleasure. For whom do you rate higher than the man who has correct beliefs about God, who has no fear of death, who has understood the purpose of Nature, who realizes that pain does not last long, and that Necessity, which some people consider the directing force of the world, is partly a matter of luck and partly in our power?

————

Gods exist, but they are not as they are popularly thought to be. To destroy the gods as they are commonly thought to be is not impious; actually it is impious to have such distorted notions. The divine powers, blessed and incorruptible, neither are troubled themselves nor do they feel anger or gratitude toward men.

————

Accustom yourself to think that death means nothing to us. For what is good and bad is a matter of sensation, and death is an end of sensation. Grasping this principle makes human life pleasant, not by giving us any promise of immortality, but by freeing us from any desire for immortality. For there is nothing in life to be afraid of for a man who understands that he need not be afraid of its extinction. So death, usually regarded as the greatest of calamities, is actually nothing to us; for while we are, death is not, and when death is here, we are not. So death means nothing to either the living or the dead, for it has nothing to do with the living and the dead do not exist.

————

Justice is a bargain based on self-interest, which we make so as to avoid being injured by others or injuring them.

SKEPTICS

During the Hellenistic period there was a development of skepticism directed at traditional religious beliefs and human pretension. The Cynic philosopher, Diogenes (c. 400-325) had set the pattern. Lucian (c. 150 A.D.), a merciless debunker, ridiculed alike the traditional gods and hypocritical men.

✐   ✐   ✐

a. DIOGENES

Diogenes walked about in the daytime with a lighted lamp, saying, "It's a good man I'm trying to find." Asked where he had met such men, he said, "Men? Nowhere. But I have met some children in Sparta."

Diogenes saw servants of Anaximenes carrying a great lot of furniture, and asked to whom it belonged. "To Anaximenes," was the reply. "Isn't he ashamed," said Diogenes, "to manage all this but not himself?"

Asked how a man can become master of himself, Diogenes replied, "By applying to himself the criticisms he makes of other people."

Diogenes said that love should be a matter of free consent, and he did not believe in marriage. Asked at what age one should marry, he said, "When young, not yet. Later—never."

Diogenes said that when he saw pilots, doctors, and philosophers he concluded that men were the wisest of creatures, but when he saw prophets and dream-interpreters and people paying heed to them, and men proud of their prestige or wealth, he thought no creatures were so ridiculous as men.

In Samothrace when a man marveled at the number of votive offerings dedicated by people who had been saved from shipwreck, Diogenes said, "There would be many more if we had the offerings of those who were not saved."

Asked what wine he liked best, he said, "Other people's."

Seeing a young man playing cottabos he said, "The better (he plays), the worse (he is)."

Asked what was his country, Diogenes replied, "I am a citizen of the world."

———

b. LUCIAN: *Zeus as Tragedian*

(*Zeus has heard that there is to be a debate on earth between a Stoic and Epicurean on the subject "Does Divine Providence Exist?" and that the Epicurean, maintaining the negative, is much the better speaker. If the negative wins, men may well cease offering sacrifices to the gods. So Zeus calls an assembly of all gods, foreign as well as Greek, to decide what to do about this critical situation. In the course of the debate, Momus, god of Criticism, speaks as follows:*)

Listen to me, Gods. I knew this would happen, that there would be agitators like this Epicurean, and I say we ourselves are to blame for it. Why blame Epicurus and his crowd for the spread of such ideas? What can we expect men to believe when everything among them is so unfair—good people suffer poverty, disease and slavery, scoundrels win prestige, wealth, and power, temple-robbers are unpunished, and it is the innocent who know best what torture means. Then we say it's a shame when a handful of sensible people declare that there isn't any Providence. We ought to be pleased that a few men will render sacrifices to us fools.

Give me a straight answer to this, Zeus. Have you ever been interested enough in mankind to separate the sheep from the goats? I'll answer for you—of course not. Providence has never bothered itself with exterminating scoundrels. Let's face the fact that we have been interested in only one thing, the size of sacrifices. I say this reckoning is just what we deserve, and men will soon realize that sacrifices and religious festivals are of no real value to them.

— Reading No. 21 —

EUCLID AND ARCHIMEDES

The Hellenistic period saw a steady development in both theoretical and practical science. Euclid (c. 300) formulated in Alexandria geometric principles and demonstrations; here are given his axioms ("things worthy of belief") and an elementary proposition. The greatest of the scientists was Archimedes of Syracuse (c. 287–212). His writings are for the most part too technical to be given here, but the picturesque accounts by Plutarch (c. 46–c. 120 A.D.) and Vitruvius (first century) will indicate his interests and his personality.

✓   ✓   ✓

a. EUCLID

Axioms.—Equals of the same thing are equal to each other. If equals be added to equals, the wholes are equal. If equals be taken away from equals, the remainders are equal. If equals be added to unequals, the wholes are unequal. If equals be taken away from unequals, the remainders are unequal. Doubles of the same thing are equal to each other. Halves of the same thing are equal to each other. The whole is greater than the part.

A Proposition (Book I, 30).—Parallels to the same straight line are also parallel to each other. Let there be AB and CD, each parallel to EF. I say that AB is also parallel to CD. For let a straight line GHI intersect them. When GHI intersects the parallels AB and EF, the angle AGI is equal to the angle GHF. Again, when GHI intersects the parallels EF and CD, the angle GHF is equal to the angle GID. It has been shown that the angle AGI is equal to the angle GHF. Therefore the angle AGI is also equal to the angle GID, and they are interchangeable. Therefore AB is parallel to CD. Therefore parallels to the same straight line are also parallel to each other. Which is precisely what had to be demonstrated.

b. ARCHIMEDES*

Now all the siege machinery which Marcellus had brought against Syracuse was worthless against Archimedes and the devices he invented, yet Archimedes set no great store by his mechanical contrivances, and, indeed, regarded them as mere gadgets whittled out by geometry in a leisure moment. But finally King Hiero, who made much of Archimedes, persuaded him to leave his theoretical reasoning for a while and turn to every-day matters: if, said he, Archimedes would apply the abstract deductions of reason to the material things perceived by the senses, he would accomplish something of great and universal value.

It was in the schools of Archytas and Eudoxus that men first began to practise this highly prized and renowned art of mechanics, which they used to lend a certain glamour and attractiveness to geometry. Moreover, some problems which could not be solved by pure reason could, at least, be illuminated by experiment and the use of mechanical devices. So, for example, with the problem of dividing a line with two mean proportionals, a construction necessary for the solution of many problems. To this they found a mechanical solution by constructing an instrument which derived the required proportions from the ratios of sections of curves.

But Plato denounced these men angrily and asserted that they were apt to corrupt and destroy the valuable part of geometry, for, he said, they were seducing this science from the immaterial and spiritual to the material and bodily, things which require much menial and brutish toil. The art of mechanics was therefore separated from the science of geometry, and for a long time was looked down on by philosophers, who regarded it as a branch of the training useful to a soldier, but nothing more. (Plutarch: *Marcellus*, 14, tr. by H. M. Howe)

––––––

The discoveries of Archimedes were many and ingenious, in widely different fields, but of them all that

* Herbert M. Howe, *Classics in Translation*, University of Wisconsin Press.

which I am now going to describe seems to me best to display his unlimited cleverness.

Since the affairs of King Hiero of Syracuse had prospered and his power had been much increased, he decided to offer a golden crown in a certain temple in thanks to the immortal gods. He therefore let out a contract to a goldsmith, to whom he paid a fee for making the crown and enough beside for the exact weight of the gold that would be necessary. At the proper time the goldsmith presented a beautifully made crown to the king, having, to judge by the weight of the crown, used all the gold that had been issued to him. But a little later the king got wind of a story that the goldsmith had abstracted some of the gold and replaced it with an equal weight of silver. Hiero was furious at having been tricked, but he saw no way to prove the theft; he therefore asked Archimedes to think over his problem.

While Archimedes was considering the matter, he went one day to the city baths. There he went into a small pool (with an overflow pipe), and while in it he reflected that the submerged part of his body made its own volume of water overflow. Realization of this showed him the principle on which his whole problem hinged, and in his delight he leaped from the pool and ran home without bothering about his clothes, anouncing in a loud voice that he had found what he was looking for. For as he hurried along he kept shouting in Greek, "I've got it! I've got it!" (Eureka! Eureka!)

The story goes on that after he had made this start he took a slab of silver and another of gold, each weighing the same as the crown. He then filled a large pot to the brim with water and dropped in the silver. Water equal in bulk to the silver ran over the edge of the pot; after removing the slab he measured the amount of water it took to refill the pot. Thus he found what weight of silver equaled that of a known bulk of water.

Next he dropped in his slab of gold, removed it, and measured the amount of water needed to replace the overflow; it was much less than had been the case with the silver—a difference corresponding to the smaller bulk of the gold, compared with the same weight of silver. Finally, he lowered in the crown, and found that

more water ran over than had done for the pure gold,
although their weights were the same. From the difference in overflows of the crown and the pure gold
Archimedes calculated the amount of silver alloyed with
the gold in the crown, and thus proved the guilt of the
goldsmith. (Vitruvius: *On Architecture*, IX, 9-12, tr.
by H. M. Howe)

———————

Let us postulate the nature of a liquid to be such
that (1) it is made up of equally distributed particles,
each in contact with its neighbors; (2) particles under
less pressure are driven aside by those under greater;
(3) each particle would be driven straight down by the
weight of the particles directly above it were it not for
the vessel which contains the liquid, or some outside
force.

Propositions

I. If any surface is cut by planes which all pass
through one fixed point, and the intersection of the
surface and any plane forms a circle, the surface is
that of a sphere whose center is the point common to
all the planes. . . . (*Archimedes gives a proof of all
these propositions, omitted here.*)

II. The surface of a liquid which is at rest is part of
the surface of a sphere whose center is the same as that
of the earth. . . .

III. If an object of the same weight as its own volume
of a liquid is lowered into the liquid until nothing pro-
trudes, it will move neither up nor down. . . .

IV. An object lighter than its own bulk of liquid will
not be completely submerged if it is lowered into the
liquid, but part will protrude above the surface. . . .

V. If an object lighter than its own bulk of a liquid
is lowered into the liquid, it will sink until the liquid
whose volume equals that of the submerged part of the
object weighs as much as the entire object. . . .

VI. If an object lighter than its own bulk of a liquid
is forced down under the liquid, it will be buoyed up by

a force equal to the difference in the weights of the
object and its volume of liquid. . . .

VII. If an object heavier than its own volume of
liquid is lowered into the liquid, it will sink to the bottom; and it will then weigh less than it did in air by an
amount equal to the weight of its own volume of liquid.

That it will sink to the bottom is apparent, for the
particles of liquid underneath the object will be pressed
harder than those at the sides, since we have described
the object as weighing more than its own volume of
liquid (*i.e.*, the object "presses down" harder than the
liquid). Now we shall show that the object becomes
lighter as indicated.

Let the rectangle with A written on it represent an object heavier than its own bulk of liquid. Let the line
marked B and C represent the weight of A, B being
the weight of liquid equal in bulk to A. We want to
prove that when A is lowered into the liquid, its weight
will equal only C.

Let us take another object D, lighter than its own bulk
of liquid, and whose weight equals B, while its volume of
liquid weighs as much as B and C together.

Now let A and D be fastened together. They will now
weigh as much as their combined volume of liquid, for
their weights together will equal the sum of their separate weights—that is, B and C added to B; and the
weight of the liquid equal in bulk to the two joined objects will equal the sum of their weights.

Accordingly, if the joined objects are lowered into the
liquid, they will float in equilibrium, moving neither up
nor down (Prop. III). It follows that A, which by itself
would sink, is being drawn *up* by D with a force equal
to its own force downward. Now since *D* is lighter than
its own bulk of liquid, it will be buoyed up by a force
equal to C, for we have shown that bodies lighter than
a liquid will, if submerged, be borne up by a force equal
to the difference between their own weights and that of
their volumes of liquid (Prop. VI). But D's volume of
liquid is heavier than D by the weight of C. It therefore
follows that A is being driven down by a force equal
to C (*i.e.*, in water A apparently loses weight B and

weighs only as much as C). (Archimedes: *On Floating Bodies,* 318-336, tr. by H. M. Howe)[1]

— Reading No. 22 —

DEFENSE AGAINST DICTATORSHIP

The orator Demosthenes (384-322) tried to arouse the Athenians to organize resistance against Philip of Macedon, but they did too little and acted too late. The following excerpts are from his Philippics.

✓   ✓   ✓

[1] Archimedes rarely uses the term *force;* he thinks in terms of gain or loss in weight. The term is used here to keep the language from being too incomprehensible. Notice, too, that he does not express the notion that every substance has its own specific gravity, although it is implied.

Archimedes' proof rests on his use of substances of reciprocal specific gravities. Suppose that we use aluminum (sp. gr. 2.7) and white pine (sp. gr. .37). Let A be a block of aluminum 100 cubic inches in volume. It will weigh about 9.7 pounds. One hundred cubic inches of water (B) will weigh about 3.6 pounds; the difference between A and B will be 6.1 pounds (C). Now let D be a block of pine weighing the same as B (3.6 pounds). It will occupy about 270 cubic inches; this much water will weigh 9.7 pounds. If the two blocks are fastened together they will weigh 13.3 pounds; the water equal to their volume will also weigh 13.3 pounds, and they will float in equilibrium. The buoyancy of the pine, then, is equal to the apparent weight of the aluminum in water; but this in turn is equal to the weight of the aluminum in air minus the weight of its own volume of water. H.M.H.

If any man supposes this to be peace, when Philip is conquering every one else and will ultimately attack you, he is mad. If we wait for him actually to declare war on us we are naïve indeed, for he would not do that even though he marched right into Attica, if we may judge from what he has done to others.

―――――

In my opinion it would be better for us to be at war with all the states of Greece, if they enjoyed democratic governments, than to be friends with them all if they were ruled by small cliques; for with free states it would not be difficult to make peace whenever you wished, but with oligarchical governments we could not even form a union on which we could rely; for it is not possible for those who exercise arbitrary power to be trustworthy friends of men who choose to live on terms of freedom and equality.

―――――

If you analyze it correctly you will conclude that our critical situation is chiefly due to men who try to please the citizens rather than to tell them what they need to hear. Some of these speakers, attempting to maintain their own popularity and power, take no thought for the future and think it is unnecessary for you to do so. Others, by accusing and slandering men who utter in public their convictions, keep the city in a state of internal strife so that Philip may be free to continue his aggressive tactics.

Under such circumstances, men of Athens, do not be angry with me if I speak to you frankly. Freedom of speech is, as you well know, the basic right of all people in Athens, even of foreigners and slaves; yet now you want to curtail it when advice on the most urgent matters is offered you. You are being ruined by yielding to flattery in meetings of the Assembly while the utmost danger is confronting you. I beg of you to hear what I have to say. I shall speak without flattery, but with your welfare my only concern.

―――――

What is the cause of this situation? There are good reasons why, whereas Greeks in former times were eager to defend their freedom, they are now willing to be slaves. My fellow countrymen, in those days the people had morale which is lacking now, morale which conquered even Persian gold and kept Greece independent, morale which refused to admit defeat on either land or sea. Then a man who was convicted of taking bribes was severely punished. But now our most precious possessions are sold like goods in the marketplace, and in exchange we have received things which spell ruin for Greece. We have, to be sure, our battleships, soldiers, a large military budget and plenty of equipment, all of these more than in those earlier times; but now everything is made ineffective because the motive of personal gain has supplanted that of patriotic devotion.

———

While a ship is still safe is the time for the pilot and sailors to be alert to make sure that no one intentionally or unintentionally capsizes it. Once the sea swamps it, effort will be wasted. So with us, men of Athens, while our city is still safe, powerful, wealthy, and glorious, we must do two things: (1) provide for our defense, with adequate equipment of ships and men, for although all other people are willing to be slaves we cannot fail to fight to remain free; (2) call upon other states to be our allies, to share the expense and the perils of preventing Philip from becoming master of the world. If you expect other states are going to save Greece while you fail to face the issue, you are making a tragic mistake. This is your task. Your ancestors, who did their duty in spite of many dangers, bequeathed this obligation to you.

FEDERAL UNION

A valiant attempt in interstate cooperation, the Achaean League, was successful within its limited sphere. The historian Polybius (c. 203–c. 120) described its constitution and paid tribute to its ablest administrator, King Aratus of Sicyon, in his Universal History.

✔   ✔   ✔

How did it happen that these states of the Peloponnesus were willing to adopt this constitution and be called Achaeans? To say it was just a matter of chance would not be an adequate explanation; it would be evading the issue. One must look for a cause, for without a cause nothing can be brought about. I believe this was the cause: nowhere could one find a more objectively fair and carefully planned constitution of equality and freedom, that is, of democracy, than among the Achaeans. Many other Peloponnesian states welcomed the opportunity of adopting it; many were persuaded to share in it; some, forced to join, soon realized its benefits. None of the original members had any special privileges, but all members had equal rights. This constitution must be regarded as the source of Peloponnesian unity and prosperity.

ARATUS. That war is terrible I grant, but it is not so terrible that we should submit to anything in order to avoid it. Why do we boast of our civic equality and freedom of speech and all that we mean by the word liberty, if nothing is preferable to peace? Peace with justice and honor is the most beautiful and profitable of possessions, but if it is allied with baseness and cowardice nothing is more shameful and disastrous.

REFUGE IN SENTIMENT

The prevailing mood of the Hellenistic world was individualism, which included a refuge in pastoral and sentimental poetry. Following are excerpts from the Idylls *of Theocritus (c. 270) and lesser lyric poets such as Meleager (c. 140–c. 70), who compiled the first anthology ("bouquet") of verse. Some of the poets represented in the complete* Greek Anthology *were much later in date, but carried on the Hellenistic tradition.*

✓   ✓   ✓

a. THEOCRITUS: *Idyll I*

(In the Sicilian sunshine the shepherd Thyrsis describes how herdsman Daphnis died of love and all nature mourned him.)

Begin, dear Muses, begin your country song. This is Thyrsis from Mount Aetna who sings so sweetly.

Where were you when Daphnis fell sick, where were you, Nymphs? Was it in the lovely vale of Peneus, or the glens of Mount Pindus or by Anapus' stream or Aetna's peak or the sacred river of Acis? *Begin, dear Muses, begin your country song.*

When Daphnis died the foxes and wolves wailed for him, and the forest lion mourned. Many were the cattle and many the bulls, many the heifers and calves who moaned for him. *Begin, dear Muses, begin your country song.*

Then Hermes came from the hills and asked, "Whom are you pining for, Daphnis, whom are you so in love with?" *Begin, dear Muses, begin your country song.*

The cowherds, the shepherds, and the goatherds came and asked what troubled him. And the god Priapus came and said, "My poor Daphnis, whom are you pining for? The girl is wandering along the glens looking for you, so lovesick and so helpless."

The herdsman made no reply, but endured to the end his bitter love. *Begin, dear Muses, begin your country song.*

Then Aphrodite came with a smile concealing her anger, and said, "You boasted that you would overcome Love, Daphnis, but has he not overcome you?" *Begin, dear Muses, begin your country song.*

Daphnis replied, "Cruel Cyprian, enemy of all mankind, so you think my life ended? I shall be Love's plague even in Hades.

.   .   .

Cease your country song, Muses, cease your country song.

Come, Pan, and take this pipe of mine, well fitted to my lip and fragrant of wax, for Love is taking me to Hades. *Cease your country song, Muses, cease your country song.*

Violets, bear briars henceforth, thistles bear violets, iris grow on the juniper tree and figs on the pine, and everything go awry, now that Daphnis is dying. Let the hind rend the hounds and the screech owls on the mountains rival the nightingales. *Cease your country song, Muses, cease your country song.*

When Daphnis had said this he spoke no more. Aphrodite would have revived him, but the thread of the Fates was utterly spun and Daphnis went down the river. Drowned by the flood was he whom the Muses loved and the Nymphs did not disdain.

———

b. THEOCRITUS: *Idyll X*

(*The scene is a field where middle-aged Milon and Bucaeus, a love-sick youth, are reaping.*)

MILON. Farmhand Bucaeus, what ails you? It's pitiful the way you can't cut your swath straight as you used to, and you can't keep up with the man next you. You're being left behind like a sheep with a thorn in her foot. If you're lagging this early, where will you be when afternoon comes and when the day is ending?

BUCAEUS. Milon, you day-long reaper and hard as a rock, have you never happened to want someone who is away?

MILON. Never! What use is wanting to a hired hand like me?

BUCAEUS. Have you never lain awake at night because of love?

MILON. No, and I hope I never will. It's a bad business for a dog to taste meat pudding.

BUCAEUS. But I, O Milon, have been in love for nearly a week and a half.

MILON. Anybody can see you draw wine from a hogshead while I don't have even enough vinegar.

BUCAEUS. So the land in front of my house hasn't been hoed since the time I put the seed in.

MILON. Which of the girls is plaguing you?

BUCAEUS. Polybota's daughter. Just the other day she was piping to the reapers at Hippocion's farm.

MILON. A god has found you out. Now you've got what you wanted so long, and a locust will cling to you all night.

BUCAEUS. So you're blaming me. But Wealth isn't the only blind one, heedless Love is another. Don't you boast.

MILON. I'm not boasting. You just keep on laying down the field, and practice a serenade to your girl. That will help you work better. I know you used to be quite a singer.

BUCAEUS. Pierian Muses, join me in singing about my slender darling, for everything you take hold of you make beautiful.

Charming Bombyca, all the people call you Gipsy, skinny and sunburned, but I call you honey-colored. The violet's dark, too, and so is the iris, but when people make bouquets those are the flowers they choose first. The goat pursues the clover, the wolf goes after the goat, the stork follows the plough, and I—I'm crazy about you! If only I owned the money they say belonged to King Croesus we'd both have gold statues of ourselves dedicated to Aphrodite—you holding pipes or a rose, or perhaps an apple, I in my best clothes and with new shoes on my feet. Charming Bombyca, your feet go tripping along like knucklebone dice, and your voice is husky-sweet, but as for your pretty ways, I can't begin to describe them.

MILON. Well, Boukos never let us know what a fine singer he is, and what a job he can do with harmony! Why was I fool enough to grow a beard? But now listen to this harvest-song of mine—

Demeter, giver of bounteous fruit and grain, make our field yield as much as honest work deserves.

Hold your sheaves tight, binders, or a passerby will say, "These are fig-wood weaklings, not worth their wages." Between the north and west winds place the straws, to let the breeze fatten the ears. For threshers, my lads, there's no napping at noon, for that's the best time for beating out the grain. But reapers get up with the lark and go to bed when he does, so it's right for them to rest in the noonday heat. If only I were a frog, lads! He leads a fine life, without a worry in the world. He needs nobody to draw his drink, there's always plenty of it right beside him. Shame on you, mess steward! Give us better beans, and don't cut your finger chopping caraway seeds in half.

That's the sort of song that men who work in the sun ought to sing. But your spindly serenade, Bucaeus, would be a fine thing to let your mother hear when she's lying in bed in the morning.

C. GREEK ANTHOLOGY

They told me, Heraclitus, of your death, and I wept as I remembered how often the two of us used to put the sun to rest with our talking. And now that you are dust, still your nightingales keep singing, for death which takes everything away can never take them. (Callimachus)

Philip laid to rest here his twelve-year old son, Nicoteles, in whom he had such hope. (Callimachus)

The garland withers about Heliodora's head, but her radiant beauty outgarlands the garland. (Meleager)

———

Within my heart the sculptor Love himself has modeled sweetly prattling Heliodora, soul of my very soul. (Meleager)

———

I send you sweet perfume, giving grace to the perfume, not to you, for you outperfume the perfume. (Anon.)

REFUGE IN SATIRE AND PESSIMISM

Another form which Hellenistic individualism took was a refuge in satire and the sense of futility. Theophrastus (c. 372–c. 285), noted chiefly for his pioneering treatise on botany, satirized types of pests in his Characters; *and Lucian, in* Timon the Misanthrope, *criticized the greed and hypocrisy of both gods and men. In the* Greek Anthology *there were many satirical and pessimistic poems.*

✓   ✓   ✓

a. THEOPHRASTUS: *Characters*

The grumbler, when a friend has sent him some food left over from a dinner, says to the bearer, "He begrudged me his thin soup and cheap wine, since he didn't invite me to the party." He is irritated with Zeus, not because it rains, but because it rains later than he wished. After finding a purse in the street he says, "I have never found a treasure." And to the person telling him "It's a boy!" he replies, "Add to that, 'Half of your property is now as good as gone,' and it's the truth you'll be saying."

———

The flatterer, when he is walking with someone, likes to say, "Do you see how admiringly men are looking at you? You are the only person in the city that this happens to. Yesterday in the marketplace you were highly praised. More than thirty people were talking about who is the best man here, and they all agreed it was you." When the man says something the flatterer orders others to be silent; he praises him, while the man is listening; and when the man makes a joke the flatterer stuffs his cloak into his mouth as if he couldn't control his laughter. When the man walks down the street the flat-

terer orders those they meet to stand until the man
passes by. He gives apples to the man's children—while
their father is watching, of course; and gives them a kiss
and says, "Chicks of a noble father." When being entertained at dinner he praises the wine, and whenever he
takes anything from the table he says, "How good this
is!" And he praises the man's house as surpassingly
beautiful and the man's idealized portrait as a perfect
likeness.

---

b. LUCIAN: *Timon the Misanthrope*

(*Timon of Athens was once wealthy and generous and
had a host of friends. Now in poverty he is trying to
make a living as a laborer on a mean little farm, and
all his friends have deserted him. He yells his criticism
of Zeus for not punishing them.*)

TIMON. O Zeus, where now are your lightning and
thunder? When you were young you took plenty of action against unjust people, and your thunderbolt was
always at work, and with floods and earthquakes you
used to punish them. But now you are easygoing, and
men dishonor you and plunder your temple, they don't
sacrifice to you any more, or crown your statues. And
before long, oh noblest of gods, they'll throw you out,
like Cronos, from your position of power. Just look at
what happened to me. I made many wretchedly poor
Athenians rich, by pouring out my wealth on them, but
now that I've become poor because of my generosity,
I'm not even recognized by those fellows. So I have taken
a leather apron and spade and work as a hired hand.
Come on now, son of Cronos, be manly and vigorous
again!

(*Zeus hears him, and asks Hermes about him.*)

ZEUS. Who is this person, Hermes, who is bawling so
from Attica? Apparently he's a poor tiller of the soil.
And a talkative chap, to boot, and, it seems, something
of a philosopher. For he keeps saying the most impious
things about us.

HERMES. What are you saying, father? Don't you
know Timon? He is that recently rich man who used to

worship us by sacrificing whole hecatombs. We used to celebrate your festival at his home in splendid fashion.

ZEUS. What a sorry change of affairs! That fine man, that wealthy one? How did he come to this condition?

HERMES. He poured out his wealth, so now he has become a poor hired hand on a farm. His previous friends pass by him without giving him a glance or knowing his name.

(*Zeus decides to send Wealth down to Timon with Hermes to guide him, since Wealth is blind. He also instructs Hermes to stop by Mount Aetna and order a Cyclops blacksmith to come to Olympus to repair Zeus' thunderbolt, which was damaged when Zeus aimed it at the atheist Anaxagoras but hit a rock instead. Hermes discovers Timon digging on his rocky farm surrounded by Poverty, Toil, Wisdom, and Manliness.*)

POVERTY. Where are you leading this fellow, Hermes?

HERMES. We've been sent to Timon by Zeus.

POVERTY. So now Wealth has been sent to Timon? Timon, the man who, after he had been ruined by Luxury I took over, and along with Wisdom and Toil made him a noble and really worthy man. I'm leaving, and you, Toil and Wisdom and the rest, follow me. Timon will soon know that he has cast off a good fellow-worker and a teacher of the best things in life. For while he associated with me he was healthy in body and vigorous in mind, he lived a man's life and scorned superficial things.

HERMES. They are leaving. Let's go to Timon.

TIMON. Who are you, you accursed ones? What are you after in coming here, bothering a working man and wage earner? Go away! And you won't be happy as you go, for I'll pelt you with rocks.

HERMES. Never do that, Timon! Please don't throw them! For it isn't men you are throwing at. I am Hermes, and this is Wealth, and Zeus sent us when he heard your prayers.

TIMON. You'll be sorry you came, even though you are gods. For I hate everybody, gods and men. And as for this blind fellow, I'll smash his head with my spade.

WEALTH. Let's go, Hermes. I think the man's crazy.

HERMES. Please don't do any such thing, Timon. But

stretch out your hands and receive good fortune and welcome Wealth.

TIMON. I have no need of you. My spade is enough wealth for me, and I am the happiest man alive when there's nobody near me. And now Poverty is my dearest friend. So go away, Hermes, and take Wealth away with you.

(*At last Timon agrees to accept Wealth, and proceeds to dig up a treasure. Then his old friends promptly re-appear with pious expressions of affection. Timon pelts them with rocks, and declares that henceforth he will live as a misanthrope—hater of mankind. Here is the encounter with one of the "friends."*)

DEMEAS. Greetings, Timon! For a long time I've been admiring and liking you, and now I've been wishing my son to meet you. I've named him Timon, after you.

TIMON. How's that, Demeas? You're not married.

DEMEAS. But I'm going to get married, and the boy that's going to be born—for it will be a boy—I am already calling Timon.

TIMON. I'm not so sure you ever will marry after I beat you up.

———

C. GREEK ANTHOLOGY

The night raven sings as a harbinger of death, but when the crooner Demophilus sings, even the night raven dies. (Nicarchus)

———

The portrait painter Eutychus had twenty sons, but even among them he never got a likeness. (Lucilius)

———

Yesterday Dr. Marcus merely touched a statue of Zeus, and although it is stone, and Zeus, its funeral is being held today. (Nicharchus)

———

Hail, seven pupils of Aristides, professor of rhetoric— four walls, three benches. (Anon.)

———

Along with five others Charmus ran the distance race, and, strange to relate, came in seventh. When there were only six, you will say, how did he come in seventh? Well, a friend of his wearing a heavy mantle ran alongside yelling, "Come on, Charmus!" So Charmus came in seventh. If he had had five more such friends he would have come in twelfth. (Nicarchus)

All Cilicians are scoundrels. But among the Cilicians there is one upright man, Cinyras, and Cinyras is a Cilician. (Demodocus)

The rose blooms only a little while. If you come by later looking for it, you will find, not a rose, but a thorn. (Anon.)

I did not exist, I was born, now I am not. That's all. If anyone shall say more he'll be lying—I shall not exist. (Anon.)

Life is a stage and a playground. Either learn to play your part gaily, or endure the suffering. (Palladas)

Here I lie, sixty-year-old Dionysius of Tarsus. I never married, and I wish my father never had. (Anon.)

Everything is absurdity, dust, nothingness. There is no meaning to existence. (Glycon)

A SHORT BIBLIOGRAPHY

GREEK AUTHORS

In the Loeb Classical Library (Cambridge: Harvard University Press) there are scholarly texts and translations of all the authors who have been cited. A comprehensive anthology of contemporary translations is P. MacKendrick and H. M. Howe, *Classics in Translation*, Vol. 1 (Madison: University of Wisconsin Press, 1952). Translations more traditional in character will be found in T. J. Oates and C. T. Murphy, *Greek Literature in Translation* (New York: Longmans, Green, 1946), and W. H. Auden, *The Portable Greek Reader* (New York: Viking, 1948).

Epic Poetry. Among the many modern translations of the *Iliad* and the *Odyssey* are the spirited ones by Samuel Butler (Princeton, N. J.: Van Nostrand).

Lyric Poetry. The best anthology is T. F. Higham and C. M. Bowra, Eds., *Oxford Book of Greek Verse in Translation* (Oxford University Press, 1938). Pindar's *Odes* have been well translated by Richard Lattimore (Chicago University Press, 1947), and R. C. Trevelyan's *Theocritus' Idylls* (Cambridge University Press, 1947) is recommended.

Drama. Excellent collections are G. Murray, etc., *Fifteen Greek Plays Translated into English* (Oxford University Press, 1943) and D. Fitts, etc., *Greek Plays in Modern Translation* (New York: Dial, 1947). The Chicago University Press is completing translations of all the tragedies, under the editorship of Richard Lattimore and David Grene.

History. The Everyman Library (New York: Dutton) translations of Herodotus (by George Rawlinson, 2 vols.) and Thucydides (by Richard Crawley) are satisfactory.

Philosophy. C. M. Bakewell, *Source Book in Ancient Philosophy* (New York: Scribner, 1907) gives a convenient summary. A standard work is J. Burnet, *Early Greek Philosophy* (London: Black, 1945). In the Everyman Library are *Socratic Dialogues of Plato and Xenophon, Five Dialogues of Plato on Poetic Inspiration,* and *Plato's Republic. Aristotle Selections* (New York: Scribner, 1927), edited by W. D. Ross, gives key portions of Aristotle's major works.

GREEK HISTORY AND INSTITUTIONS

AGARD, W. R., *What Democracy Meant to the Greeks,* Chapel Hill: University of North Carolina Press, 1942.

BARKER, E., *Greek Political Theory: Plato and His Predecessors,* London: Methuen, 1947.

BOTSFORD, G. W. and ROBINSON, C. A., *Hellenic History,* New York: Macmillan, 1948.

BURY, J. B., *A History of Greece,* New York: Modern Library, 1937.

DODDS, E. R., *The Greeks and the Irrational,* Berkeley: University of California Press, 1951.

GARDINER, E. A., *The Art of Greece,* London: The Studio, 1925.

GLOTZ, G., *The Greek City and Its Institutions,* New York: Knopf, 1930.

JAEGER, W., *Paideia: The Ideals of Greek Culture* (3 vols.) New York: Oxford University Press, 1939-44.

LIVINGSTONE, R. W. (Ed.), *The Legacy of Greece,* Oxford University Press, 1942 (excellent chapters on science and politics).

MURRAY, G., *Five Stages of Greek Religion,* Boston: Beacon Press, 1951.

NILSSON, M. P., *History of Greek Religion,* Oxford University Press, 1949.

NORWOOD, G., *Greek Comedy,* Boston: Luce, 1949.

NORWOOD, G., *Greek Tragedy,* London: Methuen, 1920.

TAYLOR, A. E., *Socrates, the Man and His Thought,* New York: Doubleday, 1953.

ZELLER, E., *Outline of the History of Greek Philosophy,* New York: Harcourt Brace, 1931.

ZIMMERN, A. E., *The Greek Commonwealth,* Oxford University Press, 1931.

INDEX

187